Books Are Essential!

A free book from BookGive,
a Denver nonprofit.

www.BookGiveDenver.org

Advance Praise for the Book

'This book is a ruthless exposure of monumental follies. What Ranganathan describes, chapter after chapter, is discrimination unparalleled in world history, in that it is directed against the majority community. And then it dawns on you that the onward march of Indian civilisation was, deliberately or otherwise, ruptured post-independence by grave injustices to the Hindus, surprising and inexplicable in equal measure as following the partition of the country along religious lines, our civilisational heritage should have naturally assumed its rightful place. Many Hindus would not even be aware of such extensive legislative, judicial and constitutional apartheid. Some deeply disturbing questions arise from this work, because while it is apparent that one regime was primarily responsible for these acts of discrimination against the majority community, why has there been no effort towards rectification under subsequent, sympathetic governments? Awareness is a necessary first step to course correction and one hopes this crisp and powerful book does exactly that.'

—Meenakshi Jain
Historian and Senior Fellow,
Nehru Memorial Museum and Library

'Powerful and evocative, drawing on historical, social and political contexts to support its arguments, this book forces the reader to question prevailing narratives and consider the implications of discriminatory practices that have reduced the Hindu to an eighth-class citizen in his own country. It challenges readers to critically examine the status quo and engage in a broader dialogue about religious freedom and equality. *Hindus in Hindu Rashtra* is a searing commentary, a manifesto of sorts for the modern Indic age. One hopes it is not reduced to just a cry in the wilderness.'

—Vishnu Jain
Lawyer and Hindu Rights Activist

Hindus in Hindu Rashtra

Hindus in Hindu Rashtra

Eighth-class Citizens and Victims of State-sanctioned Apartheid

Anand Ranganathan

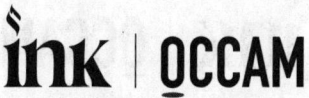

Copyright © 2023 Anand Ranganathan

Anand Ranganathan asserts his rights under the Indian Copyright Act
to be identified as the author of this work.

All rights reserved under the copyright conventions. No part of this publication may
be reproduced or transmitted in any form or by any means, electronic or mechanical,
including photocopying, recording or any information storage or retrieval system,
without the prior permission in writing from the publisher.

This book is solely the responsibility of the author(s) and the publisher has had no
role in the creation of the content and does not have responsibility for anything
defamatory or libellous or objectionable.

BluOne Ink Pvt. Ltd does not have any control over, or responsibility for, any third-party
websites referred to in this book. All internet addresses given in this book
were correct at the time of going to press. The author and publisher regret any
inconvenience caused if addresses have changed or sites have ceased to exist, but
can accept no responsibility for any such changes.

ISBN: 978-93-92209-47-5

First published in India 2023
This edition published 2025

BluOne Ink Pvt. Ltd
A-76, 2nd Floor, Sector 136, Noida
Uttar Pradesh 201301
www.bluone.ink
publisher@bluone.ink

Printed and bound in India by Thomson Press (India) Ltd

Kali and Occam are imprints of BluOne Ink

Contents

	Foreword	ix
	Prologue	xv
1	State Control of Hindu Temples	1
2	Injustice towards Kashmiri Hindus	11
3	The Waqf Act, 1995	27
4	The RTE Act	43
5	Legislations that Appease Non-Hindus but Target Hindus	55
6	Judiciary that Almost Exclusively Tries to Reform Hinduism	67
7	Celebrating Those Who Killed and Converted Millions of Hindus	80
8	Places of Worship Act, 1991	91
	Epilogue	105
	Afterword	109

Notes and References   113
Acknowledgements   129
Index   131

Foreword

For far too long, 'independent India' has not allowed the followers of its indigenous Bharatiya faith systems—the Hindus—the right to hold grievances, much less air them. After all, we are told, Hindus are in the majority, so what possible grievances could we have? Despite the bloody partition of our sacred geography—Bharat—on avowedly religious lines in 1947, Hindus are told that being in the majority is sin enough, which requires constant and unequivocal expressions of contrition in every sphere to reassure some minorities (those who identify themselves with Islamic invaders, settler colonisers and Christian European colonisers) of their safety and dignity. This reassurance, as Dr Anand Ranganathan rightly points out in this book, takes two forms: the 'positive', through political appeasement of minorities and the 'negative', through 'legal' yet unconstitutional discrimination of Hindus. As Anand bluntly observes in the book, while political appeasement continues unabated even under the current dispensation, it is the entrenched discrimination against Hindus, through the instrumentality of the law, that causes greater and long-term harm to the survival of Hindus. Accordingly, in this book, as a cultural Hindu, Anand has pressed into service his scientific bent of mind and formidable powers of analysis to identify eight illustrations of discrimination against Hindus in a Hindu-majority country, discrimination that continues under a supposedly pro-Hindu dispensation.

From State control of Hindu religious institutions to arming a predatory and expansionist mindset with the Waqf Act of 1995, to denial of the Kashmiri Hindu Holocaust, to perpetual and relentless 'reformist' scrutiny of the Hindu way of life, to State endorsement of continuing Islamic triumphalism through the Places of Worship Act of 1991, Anand has chosen to lend his powerful voice to the ongoing Sanatani

Movement for reclamation of Dharmic identity and space. In his inimitable style, through these examples, which are dealt with crisply and with substantiation, Anand has demonstrated the central thesis of his exposition—that Hindus were and continue to be eighth-class citizens regardless of who holds the reins of power, and that tokenism without long-term policy change is being used to keep the community in good humour. Understandably, to a non-Abrahamic indigenous community, which is an unconscious global minority and a deliberately fragmented national majority, any political option that merely vocalises its interests *without* effecting a policy change *despite* wielding power, must come across as a breath of fresh air.

However, given the increasing active 'legal' encroachment and simultaneous comatose cession of Hindu space, both physical and mental, the time has come to call a spade a spade, and expect concrete steps to undo the continuing damage to Hindu interests. This book, which acts as a primer on the specific issues eating into the vitals of the Hindu community, is a must-read. It serves as a fantastic starting point for those who wish to delve deeper into each of the issues enumerated by Anand, and issues that are either related or of a similar nature. I thank Anand for undertaking this task and for adding to the growing literature of Indic/Dharmic Renaissance. I wish this book all success and I hope it awakens, re-awakens, more hearts and minds.

J. Sai Deepak
Advocate, Supreme Court of India

Prologue

Ever since Mahatma Gandhi succeeded in controlling this nation's pulse, we have witnessed minority appeasement on an unprecedented scale—sometimes as virtue signalling, at other times as placation of victimhood. To illustrate but one instance of the extent to which he was committed to realising his warped vision, while preaching to those affected by the pre-partition Hindu–Muslim violence, he urged: 'Hindus should not harbour anger in their hearts against Muslims even if the latter wanted to destroy them. Even if the Muslims want to kill us all, we should face death bravely. If they established their rule after killing Hindus, we would be ushering in a new world by sacrificing our lives.'[1]

Right from the Khilafat Movement to the cushioning of the Moplah massacre,[2] to the Rangila Rasool incident,[3] to blatantly discriminatory State and Central articles and amendments, to school curriculums, to Haj subsidy, to ignoring the Prohibition of Child Marriage Act, to Shah Bano, to the declaration by a sitting prime minister that minorities have the first right to resources[4]—every single time the minority has been appeased, it has only emboldened their leaders and political fronts for further extortion and blackmail. This has come at an enormous cost—not only for their own community but also for the Hindus.

The question, though, is not of appeasement. Yes, appeasement is discriminatory—of course it is—but worse than appeasement is the active discrimination against the community not being appeased. Worse than appeasement of one community is apartheid against other communities. Truth be told, appeasement may rankle, but Indians have learnt to accept it, even take it in their stride, for they realise the reasons for appeasement are political, and those reasons are mollification of vote banks to win elections. Every political party, cutting across ideologies and religious affiliations or labels, indulges in appeasement. So while our Muslim population is 14.2 per cent, in the last eight years, as many as 31.3 per cent of homes under the Awaas Yojna, 33 per cent of funds under the Kisaan Sammaan Nidhi Yojna and 36 per cent of loans under the Mudra Yojna have gone to the Muslims.[5] The BJP government has a Pradhan Mantri Shadi-Shagun Scheme exclusively for Muslim girls who complete their graduation before marriage. They will get ₹51,000, no questions asked.[6] Housing, skilling, scholarships, *sarkari* jobs, salaries to maulvis—there is appeasement and preferential treatment meted out to minorities by every political party including the BJP.[7] The BJP recently even offered Christian senior citizens a free trip to Jerusalem if they voted for it.[8] Fact is, Ram Rajya and Rome Rajya are interchangeable, depending upon which way the wind is blowing.

No, the issue, I repeat, is not of appeasement. The issue is of apartheid. The issue is of State-sponsored, State-sanctioned discrimination against a particular community. And that community is the majority community—the Hindus. This work concerns not appeasement but apartheid. It concerns not dignity but discrimination that is now so entrenched in our Constitution, our policies, our legal framework, our society and our psyche, that it makes Hindus not just second-class citizens but, rather, eighth-class citizens. That this is happening in the so-called Hindu Rashtra is profoundly ironical. Here, then, are eight reasons why Hindus are eighth-class citizens in their own country.

1
State Control of Hindu Temples

State control of Hindu temples and their property is by far the largest, financially most damaging scam of independent India. That it not only continues but flourishes under the present government is a sad reflection of how politicians in our country treat Hindus. Even using the petroleum sector as a cash cow pales in comparison to the loot and pillaging of Hindu temples. I do not know how and why it is beyond the limits of comprehension of the flagbearers of secularism, that if you truly believe that religion should be kept out of the State, the corollary is equally applicable—that the State should be kept out of religion. But is it? Secularism is total separation of religion and State. Total. There are half a dozen articles and amendments and directive principles in our Constitution that make it plural, not secular. In fact, the word secular was inserted in our preamble by Indira Gandhi during the Emergency.[9] It was absent from Ambedkar's Constitution. Our State declares itself to be secular but is shamelessly not so, regulating, governing, and controlling, as it does Hindu places of worship.

Hindu temples have been, for thousands of years, the centres of worship, learning, community living, trade and economy, statecraft and even defence. Every invader has known, that to dismantle India, you need to first dismantle this temple ecosystem. And every invader has managed it. What sets the British apart is that they managed to also pass this dismantling on to those who they ruled and subjugated; and now the latter are continuing with the dismantling. Right from the Madras Regulation VII 1817 to the Religious Endowments Act 1863, to the Religious and Charitable Endowments Act 1925, to the Hindu Religious & Endowments Act 1927, to Act XII 1935, to the post-Independence Hindu Religious and Charitable

Endowments Act 1951—Hindus have been at the receiving end of State-sponsored loot and pillaging of their places of worship. And when the 1951 legislation was challenged in the Madras High Court, and subsequently the Supreme Court, and most of the draconian provisions of the 1951 act struck down,[10] the Congress, that was in power then, quickly passed the Hindu Religious & Charitable Endowments Act 1959,[11] snubbing the court decree. Two years ago, the same Madras High Court dismissed a petition challenging the constitutional validity of this act, commenting that: 'Management of temples has got nothing to do with the right to worship. A Hindu can worship as much as he wants.'[12]

But I ask you, if the Congress can bring in a legislation to control Hindu temples, one that still stands, why cannot the present government bring in a legislation to free Hindu temples? A petition by Swami Parmatmananda and Swami Dayananda Saraswati is pending in the Supreme court since 2012.[13] *For more than 10 years*. They can allow midnight hearings for granting mercy to terrorists but cannot spare time for this. In his plea, Swamiji gave the example of the grand Ardhanareswara Temple in Tiruchengode, Tamil Nadu. Even though the temple generates more than a crore in annual income, the budget earmarked for conducting daily puja and performing rituals is a mere 1 lac.[14] Swami Dayananda Saraswati did not live to see the day his beloved temples would be wrested from State control. He passed away in 2015.

Governments of just 10 states control more than 110,000 Hindu temples. Tamil Nadu Temple Trusts own 478,000 acres of temple land.[15] Tamil Nadu government alone controls 36,425 temples and 56 mutts[16]; for Karnataka, the figure is 34,563.[17] Is this what we call secularism? The communist State of Kerala has five Devaswom boards—Travancore, Guruvayur, Cochin, Malabar and Koodalmanikyam. Together they manage 3,058 temples.[18] The communists, for whom religion is supposedly the 'opium of the masses', are controlling Hindu temples and their boards, appointing board members on their whims and fancies. Many either belong to the communist party or are card-carrying members of it.[19] Why? What business is it of the State to levy an administrative charge from anywhere between 5 per cent to 21 per cent on Hindu temples in the name of audit?[20] What business is it of the State to dictate how many times a pooja is to be conducted and who is to conduct it, and who is qualified to be the priest and what is going to be the procedure for worship?[21] What business is it of the State to control tens of thousands of acres of temple land and then set rent for it? The loss to Hindu temples on account of this alone is estimated over decades to be in lacs of crores. According to the activist and litigant T.R. Ramesh, the Tamil Nadu government, that should be earning a minimum of 6,000 crores per annum from the 2.44 crore square feet of temple land it controls, earns a mere 58 crores, not even 1 per cent.[22] Kapaleeswarar Temple is one of the richest temples in Tamil Nadu, owning more than 600 acres of prime property in Chennai. State records show it has 473 defaulters, with most of its land now encroached.[23] And these are the estimates of only one state. Because of this loss in revenue generation, Hindu temples are not able to spend money on what they would really like to spend money on—opening up ved pathshalas, schools, colleges, gaushalas, fellowships and scholarships, orphanages, Hindu cultural and religious centres—all things and causes other religions and their places of worship spend their money on unencumbered.

Only in India can you step aside and watch as the State appoints non-Hindus— Muslims like Firhad Hakim,[24] Christians like Vangalapudi Anita[25]—on boards that control Hindu temples; only here will we remain silent as temple idols are stolen, temple property auctioned, a whole temple-driven ecosystem and way of life dismantled. Assault on temples has turned into an assault on Hinduism itself. Imagine a Hindu priest or a politician controlling and dictating how St Frances Church or the Jama Masjid should be run. If that happens, perhaps our judiciary would indeed conduct a midnight hearing, crying death of secularism.

What is amusing is that the very same people who derisively call India a Hindu Rashtra are totally silent on State control of Hindu places of worship. They never stop to ask how on earth is this secularism. You can provide Haj subsidy for decades, use taxpayers' money to host grand Iftar parties, fund AMU that has only 1.4 per cent Dalit students and 0.25 per cent Dalit teachers, plunder State coffers to pay monthly salaries to tens of thousands of maulvis, ask government-run UGC to fund minority institutions that keep 50 per cent seats reserved for Christians, step in to overturn a Supreme Court judgment just to appease Muslims, leech thousands of crores exclusively from Hindu temples, control tens of thousands of acres of Hindu temple land, spend hundreds of crores of taxpayers' money for the Kartarpur corridor—are these not instances of the State interfering or succumbing to the demands of religion? Is this secularism?

The great Mahakaleshwar Temple, its revenue, its realty, is tightly controlled by the Madhya Pradesh State government through the Mahakaleshwar Mandir Act

1982[26]—from appointing *pujaris* down to even the size of the *prasadam* laddu. Down south, Tirupati's *hundi* collections from April to September 2022 alone amount to 782 crores.[27] Now the government valuation of its properties is out—7,123 acres valued at 85,705 crores.[28] But secularism means this temple comes under the Religious Institutions and Charitable Endowments Act. Until a high court order that was issued recently, Andhra Pradesh Hindu Religious Institutions Act used to force temples that earn 5 lakh or more to pay 21.5 per cent of their income to the Endowments Department.[29] Now, the State has issued orders to set up the Dharmika Parishad with draconian powers to form temple trust boards and extend land lease.[30] Is this secularism?

More than two years have gone by since the Tamil Nadu government informed the Madras High Court that 11,999 temples under its control do not have enough money to perform even a single pooja.[31] But then again, I ask—largely overriding the Supreme Court verdict, if the Congress can bring in a legislation to control Hindu temples in 1959, one that still stands, why could not the present government bring in a legislation to override it in the last nine years? Why has it brought in even more Hindu temples under State control than was achieved by the previous dispensation?

Why does the present government gloat on constructing temple corridors like the one in Kashi at the cost of 339 crores when it could have relinquished control over Hindu temples and allowed the latter to fund hundreds of such corridors over the length and breadth of this country? As far as I am concerned, a Hindu temple should be publicly listed as a company. After all, it supplies a product that people buy—peace of mind and reassurance— and unlike other companies that need to constantly refine or come up with better products, a temple's product has not changed in a millennium, and never will. Indians should be able to buy stake in it and make the temple richer. The richer it becomes through public trading, the more it will do for the society—schools, hospitals, roads, orphanages, housing, the list goes on. The more it does for the society, the more it will garner donations. With temples being publicly listed, the ready excuse of the government that, who will control the temple after we relinquish control, becomes untenable. Let the government tax the temple's wealth—no issues with that. At least, the wealth generated by the temple will belong to the temple. At least, then, the Hindus will not be so blatantly discriminated in their own country.

2
Injustice towards Kashmiri Hindus

Terrorists are targeting Hindus settled in Kashmir but not the Hindus visiting Kashmir. Tourist footfall in Kashmir this past year has been the highest ever—a staggering 16 million.[32] Business is booming. Registers are ringing. Tourists are safe.

They want the Hindus to flee but then return later as tourists. They want the Hindus to come as tourists and fill their coffers but not settle in their own land. As Sushil Pandit, a Kashmiri Hindu and himself a victim of ethnic cleansing, says—'Tourism in Kashmir funds Jihad. The Hindus are funding their own demise.' How on earth can we watch this unfold and not do anything about it? What kind of a country is this where one can settle 5,700 Rohingya Muslims[33] in Jammu and

Kashmir, but not 7 lakh Kashmiri Hindus—the original inhabitants of the land? There is no other way of saying it—we live in a nation of broken mirrors, where you possess neither a shadow nor a reflection if you are a Kashmiri Hindu. We live in a nation that waits for death to rid us of our remembrances. Please wait a little more, just a little.

Thirty years have gone, but we haven't progressed from those ugly, inhospitable transit camps that dot the Kashmir landscape at Sheikhpora, Natnusa, Veerwan, Vessu, Mattan and Hawl. In Anantnag's Vessu transit camp, Kashmiri Hindus, who want to flee because they fear for their lives, are being kept locked up. They cannot even step out to buy essentials like milk and medicines.[34] Is this the kind of freedom promised to the natives of the land, while the Rohingyas enjoy unfettered movement in the near vicinity? According to the data from the Home Ministry, only 17 per cent of the promised houses for Kashmiri Hindus have been completed in the last six years.[35] Only 5,928 Kashmiri Hindus have been appointed through the Prime Minister's Job Scheme.[36] The number of Kashmiri Hindu refugees is 700,000—a figure derived from the data provided by the Government of India, Ministry of Home Affairs. It states that 62,000 families fled Kashmir in the aftermath of the Kashmiri Hindu Genocide—a woeful underestimate given that these are government figures of registered families tabulated to provide relief and rehabilitation.[37]

To an extent, *The Kashmir Files*, a recent film by Vivek Agnihotri, has tried to reset the Kashmiri Hindu narrative, and that is why so many are rattled by it. Many prominent Kashmiri voices, politicians, intellectuals, writers and poets—all those who stayed silent even as the Kashmiri Hindu genocide unfolded right before their eyes—called for a ban on the film. To them I ask—can there be reconciliation without remembrance? Crime without comeuppance? Can there be death without deliverance? Can there be justice without Nuremberg? Why do they want to hide the truth about the Nadimarg massacre that the film truthfully depicts, where terrorist Zia Mustafa lined up 23 unsuspecting Kashmiri Hindus and shot them point blank, and as he was escaping, he heard a baby cry and his comrade goaded *'ye karnawun chupe'* and then the baby became the 24th victim.[38] Why do they want to hide this? Why do they want to hide the truth about Girija Tickoo, who was raped and cleaved in two by a mechanical saw while she was still alive?[39] Why do they want to hide the truth about B.K. Ganjoo, who hid inside a rice barrel when jihadis came looking for him after his Muslim neighbour informed on him?[40] Ganjoo was shot dead. Rice laced with his blood was fed to his wife. Why do they want to hide the truth about slogans raised from mosques on 19 January 1990—*'Ralive, Tsalive, Galive'* [convert, run or die]; 'Death to kafirs'; 'Pandits go but leave your women behind'; *'Nizam-e-Mustafa!'*[41] Why do they want to hide all this?

And what is this other side of the genocide that they demand should also be shown? Yasin Malik, the assassin of Squadron leader Khanna,[42] loved *dum aloo*? Bitta Karate, the killer of 42 Kashmiri Hindus,[43] was the son of a shawl weaver? Zia Mustafa, the perpetrator of the Nadimarg massacre, was a compounder at a hospital? I will tell you why they want this truth to be hidden. Because they realise that *The Kashmir Files* is not just a film, it is a Proustian collection of memories. Of Girija. Of Ganjoo. Of Dinanath. Of tens of thousands of Kashmiri Hindus who were betrayed by their own friends. But they forget. They might have taken away from the Kashmiri Hindus their home, but they can never take away from them their words. For their entrapment in a film may fool us into believing they have a physical form, a form that can be destroyed when the film is destroyed. But the words existed much before their prisons did. Words never die. They always survive. In times of terror, we wrap them and hide them like our ancestors did, and it may take 30 or 300 or 3,000 years for them to be uttered again—but uttered again they will be. And when they are, their words will echo in the valleys of violence where people only know how to light Molotov—these words will make them light diyas again. To be sure, I do not care about Islamists and the politicians forgetting those words. What bothers me is that our government, our judiciary, our society have forgotten them. How can these pillars of our democracy forget the cries of Girija and the laments of Dinanath? How? Hearing them, those words, those haunting voices, one feels lost for hope, wondering whether that fabled arc of moral universe would ever bend towards justice for Kashmiri Hindus. Remember that five years ago, the Supreme Court rejected reopening cases of criminal atrocities against Kashmiri Hindus because too much time had elapsed.[44] You read it right—justice is now weighed against time. Elapsed time is elapsed justice. In December of 2022, the Supreme Court reiterated its previous stand of not opening cases of atrocities against Kashmiri Hindus.[45]

It not just the Supreme Court of India that is apathetic to the misery of Kashmiri Hindus. The misery is compounded by the rubbing of salt on the wounds of the victims by appeasing and eulogising separatist leaders like Syed Shah Geelani. From journalists to politicians to judges to intellectuals, anyone who has had anything to say or do about the Kashmir problem has had to break bread with this man, knowing fully well that he was equally responsible for the Kashmiri Hindu genocide and ethnic cleansing. He was feted unceasingly while he was alive, and he is fondly remembered even in death. Geelani was responsible for pushing Kashmir into religious fanaticism, communal bigotry, genocide, Hindu exodus and untold misery. A man is known and understood best by his own words. So let me quote the words of Geelani from his book *Nava-e-Hurriyat*: (a) India is a bigger enemy of Islam and Muslims than even Israel; (b) Muslims are a *qaum* wholly separate from the Hindus. Muslims are a complete separate nation on the basis of their religion, culture, civilisation, customs and practices, and thought. Their nationalism and the foundation of their unity cannot be based on their homeland, race, language, colour or economic system. The basis of their unity is Islam and Islam alone; (c) Pakistan was created for the hegemony of Islam and for establishing an Islamic system. Pakistan is the land of the dreams of all Kashmiris because it was won in the name of Islam; (d) Accession to India would result in the Kashmiri Muslims having to live perpetually under Hindu slavery. The entire struggle of the Kashmiri people is for the sake of Islam and for accession to Pakistan; (e) Kashmir must become an Islamic State. Our goal is the establishment of Islamic government. Our struggle is for the sake of Islam; (f) Islam removes people from the slavery of people, but secularism makes the people slaves of Delhi. The on-going struggle against Indian rule in Kashmir is not an ordinary war, but, rather, a jihad; (g) I plead with the Afghan mujahidin to come forward to help liberate us from India and, by doing so, express their bond of Islamic brotherhood and religious commitment; (h) In the light of the Quran, it has now become incumbent on the people of Pakistan to engage in jihad in Kashmir. In fact, participating in the Kashmir jihad is now a binding duty incumbent not just on the Pakistani Muslims but, rather, the entire worldwide Muslim ummah.⁴⁶ These words of Geelani give you a glimpse into his world—a world full of hatred for India and Hindus. I am very clear. If you eulogise him or mourn him, you can never be trusted; your allegiance does not lie with India; your allegiance does not lie with your own people, who have been ethnically cleansed and subjected to untold suffering and genocide.

And when we speak of allegiance, we must not shirk away from the reality—that every politician at the Centre, be it from the Congress or the Janata Dal or the BJP, has flirted with those in Kashmir whose allegiance has always been suspected. Truth be told, Kashmir has been turned into a snake-and-ladder game. The ladders are provided by Pakistan and the snakes by Indians. I say Indians but I wonder if these people think of themselves as Indians. Their first allegiance is to religion, second to Pakistan, third to China and fourth to dynasty. It is a fact that Hyderabad could so easily have been what Kashmir is today—and fools in the media would be writing column yards on its 'Struggle'—but for one man—Sardar Patel. And Kashmir could so easily have been what Hyderabad is today but for two men—Nehru and Sheikh Abdullah. They set the board down for the snake-and-ladder game, which their progenies have been playing ever since, making sure Kashmir's bubbling and ever-present communal bigotry, ethnic cleansing, terrorism and religious fanaticism do not enter the India narrative. They talk of human and religious rights, but when have you heard them speak out on the atrocities committed by Pakistan against the Ahmadiyyas or the Baluchs, leave aside the Hindu and Christian minorities? When have you heard them speak out against China that has interned more than a million Uighur Muslims in concentration camps and is feeding them pork?[47] When have you heard them speak out against the brutal trampling of human rights of lakhs of Dalits, Gurkhas, women, Sikhs, refugees, and homosexuals in Kashmir because of Articles 370 and 35A? But I will tell you when they do speak out—when their power and authority are threatened. Like when Sheikh Abdullah spoke out and claimed self-determination was his right and countries that did not support it were his enemies. Or when Farook Abdullah spoke out, and I quote: 'They want to abolish 370, and we'll remain silent? Inshallah we will fight. We dare them. Allah would want that we gain independence from India.' And when it comes to the dynast Ms Mehbooba Mufti, one would be hard pressed to find a bigger hypocrite. From choosing a rape-accused as an election candidate to threatening 'rivers of blood' if 370 was abrogated, to shedding tears and mourning the death of terrorist Wani, to saying flags other than the tricolour will fly if 370 was abrogated, to threatening sedition by saying, 'Why would a Muslim majority state want to stay with India', to wanting to introduce punishment according to sharia law, like death by stoning, in Kashmir—Ms Mufti has scaled all methane spewing landfill summits. For Kashmiri Hindus to expect any sympathy or help from such leaders and their governments is, quite frankly, self-defeating. Governments come and go, and we shout, and we make a hundred excuses, but we can't get away from the fact that Kashmiri Hindus are in exile. As Salman Rushdie expressed so poignantly in the *Satanic Verses*: 'An exile is a dream of glorious return; it is an endless paradox: looking forward but always looking back. An exile is a ball hurled high into the air. He hangs there, frozen in time, translated into a photograph; denied motion, suspended impossibly above his native earth, he awaits the inevitable moment at which the photograph must begin to move, and the earth reclaim its own.'

When will that photograph begin to move? Mind turns numb at the very thought that a nation is going about its business for 30 years while half a million Hindus have been reduced to refugees in their own land. Is this what a so-called Hindu Rashtra is supposed to do for Hindus? We are the only country in the world that allows this, across parties, across governments—right or left or centre.

Three years to 2019, 3,686 law and order incidents occurred in Kashmir. Three years since 2019, the number is only 438.⁴⁸ Terror attacks have reduced by more than 40 per cent since 2018.⁴⁹ But then, why is it that only 5,000 Kashmiri Hindus have been brought home? And of those few who have been, more than 25 have lost their lives through targeted killings and assassinations. Making *The Kashmir Files* tax-free was great, but remember your dharma—it is to make sure 7 lakh Kashmiri Hindus are brought home.

Every year on 19 January, Shri Utpal Kaul, a Kashmiri Hindu activist and father of journalist Aditya Raj Kaul, brings out from underneath his mattress a crumpled piece of paper. It is a bus ticket. With a date on it. The date is 19 January 1990. Every year he does that. And every year Aditya shows it to me.⁵⁰ And I have always wondered, what does it mean for a father to have kept a bus ticket for 33 years? Is it to remind himself of that horrific journey, of his clasping tight his wife and a month-old Aditya being smuggled out in a jute bag, while he sat lost thinking of all that he had left behind? Was it to remind himself how he was counting every passing minute, counting every passing milestone to safety? Was it to remind himself of that blurred instant in the bus that contained within it the image of his struggles ahead? Or was it to remind himself that he needed to be strong, that this was a cruel, unforgiving country, that his struggles were his alone and that he would have to fight them all by himself? Was that bus ticket kept under his mattress all this while; did that bus ticket take the weight of his unbound sorrow every night of every day of every month of every year since 19 January 1990?

No.

He kept it to remind himself that from now on, in his mind, that bus ticket was his adversary, and he shall look at him straight in the eye, and tell him that he was down but not out, that he was undefeated, that he shall pick himself up, and find work and educate his children, and bring food to the table and greet every new day as he did the last—with a smile on his face; that he shall not be conquered. And on the appointed day, on 19 January, when the father slips his hand under the mattress and finds the bus ticket and hands it to his son, he could almost have said: 'Son, I pass this on to you now; it is yours; now you take care of it; for it must be preserved for our future generations. They must never forget that a man's body may be forced to flee but never his spirit. They must never forget who we are and where we came from. We are Kashmiri Hindus, son, and we stand. Today. On our feet. And one day we shall take the journey back home.'

Time is running out. A refugee accepts his fate and the humiliation that comes along with it, for he must worry about his new life. He forgets how to complain. And that is a fatal mistake. Arundhati Roy, that totem of the Left, once cushioned the crimes of the Maoists by calling them 'Gandhis with guns'. Well, Kashmiri Hindus are the Gandhis without guns, and that is the singular reason why no one cares for their plight. Because this nation hears complaints through the barrel of a gun, not the ink of a pen. This nation believes inaction is a medicine. It believes time heals. It believes wounds do not fester. It believes the exiled never return. This nation waits for death to rid its people of their remembrances. This nation wishes the Kashmiri Hindus all happiness and joy in the afterlife.

Kashmiri Hindus are the Jews, but unfortunately, India is not Israel. They call Kashmir the Switzerland of the East. Wrong. It is the Srebrenica of the East. And it will remain so till such time every Kashmiri Hindu is returned home.

3

The Waqf Act, 1995

Waqf is the third-largest landowner in India,[51] after Defence and the Railways, with much of its landholding, rather amusingly, pre-independence—an endowment of the insidious give and take between the British and the Muslims they desired to pacify. Indeed, many of the Waqf landholdings go as far back as 1857.[52] Seventy-seven per cent of Delhi is on Waqf land,[53] including the Delhi High Court. Central Vista, which has recently been renovated, and on whose hallowed turf new government buildings will shimmer and glisten, is on Waqf land. CGO Complex and Jawaharlal Nehru Stadium are on Waqf land.[54] Only three things are certain in an Indian's life—death, taxes, and that, knowingly or unknowingly, he ends up walking every day on Waqf land.

Over time, many of these Waqf properties were taken over by the government, but then, inexplicably, or perhaps not, one of the last decisions of the outgoing UPA government in 2014 was to gift 123 prime Central Delhi properties to Waqf and withdraw its claim on them.[55] These prime real estate properties are from the time of our independence and were endowed to the government by the departing British. Their status remained unchanged for 70 years, until 5 March 2014, when the departing Congress decided to endow them to the Waqf.[56] Even the Delhi High Court judges have opined that Waqf land is Allah's and Allah's alone and that the government cannot be the owner of this land.[57] It is not just government buildings that the Waqf claims to be its property; Mukesh Ambani's house is on Waqf land.[58]

The Waqf Board lays claim to 354,913 estates and 866,035 properties comprising 802,000 acres of Indian land, with UP having the highest share of 213,833 Sunni

Waqf Board properties and 15,386 Shia Waqf Board properties.[59] This data is from the Waqf Management System of India whose motto, if you visit their website, is *Once Waqf, always Waqf*.

One will, if they were to dig deeper, find that this grandiose motto is not the idea or thinking of the Waqf Board or any of its members. It is, in fact, the verbatim exclamation of the Supreme Court in its 1998 judgment, case no. 4372 SCR 398. And the name of the hon'ble judge who said this iconic line? Justice Dr Anand.[60]

Waqf essentially means that any donated property belongs to Allah, in perpetuity. Waqf decides any property adjudged by Muslim law as pious, religious or charitable and, therefore, fit to be labelled as Waqf. In other words, Waqf is inalienable and irrevocable. If you think this is a figment of my fertile imagination, let me quote directly from a Waqf Board document: 'Waqf is a voluntary, permanent and irrevocable dedication of a portion of one's wealth, in cash or kind, to Allah. Once a Waqf, it never gets gifted, inherited or sold. It belongs to Allah and the corpus of the Waqf always remains intact. The fruits of the Waqf may be utilised for any shariah-compliant purpose.'[61]

The Waqf Boards are, in case you were wondering, headed and constituted exclusively by Muslims.[62] If that was not discriminatory enough, let me run you through some sections of the Waqf Act, 1995.

Section 4 bestows on the Waqf survey commissioner the authority and power like that of a civil court.[63] Besides, the entire cost of the surveying is to be borne by the State. So, in essence, a Hindu's property, once declared as Waqf property, wholly arbitrarily, will be surveyed by Waqf, and the cost incurred on this count will be paid for by that Hindu taxpayer. And people say we are living in a fascist Hindu Rashtra.

Section 40 gives the Waqf power to decide if your land is Waqf or not.[64] In fact, if your property is laid claim to by Waqf, it is your responsibility to disprove its claim. And till such time you disprove it, it is Waqf land. 'Decision if a property is Waqf property—(1) The Board may itself collect information regarding any property which it has reason to believe to be Waqf property and if any question arises whether a particular property is Waqf property or not, or whether a Waqf is a Sunni Waqf or a Shia Waqf, it may, after making such inquiry as it may deem fit, decide the question. (2) The decision of the Board on a question under sub-section (1) shall, unless revoked or modified by the Tribunal, be final. (3) Where the Board has any reason to believe that any property of any trust or society registered in pursuance of the Indian Trusts Act, 1882 or under the Societies Registration Act, 1860 or under any other Act, is Waqf property, the Board may, notwithstanding anything contained in such Act, hold an inquiry in regard to such property and if after such inquiry the Board is satisfied that such property is Waqf property, call upon the trust or society, as the case may be, either to register such property under this Act as Waqf property or show cause why such property should not be so registered provided that in all such cases notice of the action proposed to be taken under this sub-section shall be given to the authority by whom the trust or society had been registered. (4) The Board shall, after duly considering such cause as may be shown in pursuance of notice issued under sub-section (3), pass such orders as it may think fit and the order so made by the Board, shall be final, unless it is revoked or modified by a Tribunal.'

Section 54 gives the Waqf the power to declare you an encroacher.[65] 'Removal of encroachment from Waqf property—(1) Whenever the Chief Executive Officer considers whether on receiving any complaint or on his own motion that there has been an encroachment on any land, building, space or other property which is Waqf property and, which has been registered as such under this Act, he shall cause to be served upon the encroacher a notice specifying the particulars of the encroachment and calling upon him to show cause before a date to be specified in such notice, as to why an order requiring him to remove the encroachment before the date so specified should not be made and shall also send a copy of such notice to the concerned mutawalli. (2) The notice referred to in sub-section (1) shall be served in such manner as may be prescribed. (3) If, after considering the objections, received during the period specified in the notice, and after conducting an inquiry in such manner as may be prescribed, the Chief Executive Officer is satisfied that the property in question is Waqf property and that there has been an encroachment on any such Waqf property, he may, make an application to the Tribunal for grant of order of eviction for removing such encroachment and deliver possession of the land, building, space or other property encroached upon to the mutawalli of the Waqf. (4) The Tribunal, upon receipt of such application from the Chief Executive Officer, for reasons to be recorded therein, make an order of eviction directing that the Waqf property shall be vacated by all persons who may be in occupation thereof or any part thereof, and cause a copy of the order to be affixed on the outer door or some other conspicuous part of the Waqf property: Provided that the Tribunal may before making an order of eviction, give an opportunity of being heard to the person against whom the application for eviction has been made by the Chief Executive Officer. (5) If any person refuses or fails to comply with the order of eviction within forty-five days from the date of affixture of the order under sub-section (2), the Chief Executive Officer or any other person duly authorised by him in this behalf may evict that person from, and take possession of, the Waqf property.'

So let me get this straight. The Waqf decides in its wisdom that a property is Waqf property; it then serves a notice to the 'encroacher'; subsequently, it takes the matter to the Waqf tribunal and the tribunal decides on the nature of the said property, and orders eviction.

The terror continues paragraph after paragraph, sections after sections. Section 85 states: 'No suit or other legal proceeding shall lie in any civil court in respect of any dispute, question or other matter relating to any Waqf, Waqf property, or other matter which is required by or under this Act to be determined by a Tribunal.'[66] In fact, even the Supreme Court declared in 2019[67] that a civil court of India has no jurisdiction in the matter of a suit pertaining to a Waqf property.

Let me remind you of the ground reality. Waqf tribunal decision can only be overturned by a long and financially draining legal process. The Waqf knows this. In a country where four crore cases are pending, harassment through legal procedure that stems from the inner offices of an all-appeasing government, executive and judiciary is a sword that is sharper and more potent than Khalid's.

How, one may then ask, has The Waqf Act, 1995, that is patently unfit to be applied to leave alone a mental asylum, has been applied to a nation of 1.3 billion people, assuming the two are not one and the same? Remember, there is nothing in the Act that safeguards the religious properties of Hindus being appropriated by the Waqf. This itself violates not only the principles of natural justice but also multiple articles of our Constitution beginning from Articles 14, 15 and 25. BJP's enfant terrible Ashwini Kumar Upadhyay recently filed a petition in the Supreme Court challenging the validity of the Waqf Act.[68] His plea was that the Waqf Board has Muslim MPs, MLAs, legislators, civil servants, lawyers and scholars as its members and they are renumerated by the taxpayer, even though the State does not collect money from Mosques. How is this secularism? The Supreme Court refused to entertain the plea and threw it out. The judge called the petition abstract.[69] That judge is now, and will remain for the next many years, the Chief Justice of India.

The mayhem continues. Here is Section 28[70] that outlines the power of the District Magistrate, Additional District Magistrate, and Sub-Divisional Magistrate to implement the directions of the Waqf Board: 'Subject to the provisions of this Act and the rules made thereunder, the District Magistrate or in his absence an Additional District Magistrate or Sub-Divisional Magistrate of a District in the State shall be responsible for implementation of the decisions of the Board, which may be conveyed through the Chief Executive Officer, and the Board may, wherever it considers necessary, seek directions from the Tribunal for the implementation of its decisions.'

Then there is Section 107.[71] Now in law, there is something called the Statute of Limitation, that is, the time period for acting on a dispute or filing of a suit is set by law, and this law is enacted through the Limitation Act, 1963. But wait. Section 107 states: 'Act 36 of 1963 will not apply for recovery of Waqf properties. Nothing contained in the Limitation Act, 1963 shall apply to any suit for possession of immovable property comprised in any Waqf or for possession of any interest in such property.'

What this means is, that the Waqf can lay claim to and recover any property it wishes to without having to worry about the passage of time. The Waqf, as you would have realised by now, is a parallel government, wholly sanctioned by our own government. It has, through its overarching board, its own legislature; through its surveyors and estate and compliance officers its own executive; and through its tribunal its own judiciary. And through this Act, through its application, a message is sent to every citizen of this country. We are a special people. And that message is all pervasive and uncompromising. It is this message that allows Muslims, even rational, logical and educated Muslims, to claim that the Gyanwapi Mosque built atop the grand Kashi Vishwanath temple is on Waqf land.[72] So, was the grand Kashi Vishwanath Temple demolished by Aurangzeb and as confirmed through his own certified biography, *Masir-e-Alamgiri*, also on Waqf land? It is this message that allows Muslims to claim that the 1,500-year-old iconic Manendiyavalli Chandrashekhara Swami Temple in Tamil Nadu is on Waqf land.[73] I ask you—how can a 1,500-year-old Hindu temple be adjudged by Waqf to be on Islamic land when Islam is only 1,300 years old?

The more you read on Waqf, the more you realise that bulk of its muscle is flexed not only through the draconian Waqf Act but also through a letter that the former prime minister, Indira Gandhi, wrote during the Emergency, ordering all states to strictly obey her dictats.[74] If the Waqf properties, she wrote, have gone into adverse possession of State government departments, the Wakf Board could well start legal proceedings against the concerned departments, and where costly buildings have been put up by the State on Waqf land and their vacation is not feasible, the State government may enter into permanent leases with Wakf Boards after paying to the Boards the bulk of the market value as premium. She further wrote that Waqf Boards have sent governments list of Waqf properties in the possession of government departments. She urged to see that these are dealt with as suggested above. A periodic review should be undertaken, and a monthly report to be sent to her. Waqf, as ordained by the Committee and as agreed to by the Centre, should be treated differently from individual landlords and, therefore, exempt from Rent Control Acts.

The Waqf only asked the Congress to bend. The Congress decided to crawl. In fact, during the dying days of the UPA, The Waqf Properties (Eviction of Unauthorised Occupants) Bill, 2014, was tabled in the Rajya Sabha, giving overarching and draconian powers to the Waqf Eviction Officer to demolish whatever it considered was an encroachment of the Waqf property.[75]

Through this tabled bill, not only was every order made by the Waqf Estate Officer to be considered final, it could also not be called into question in any original suit or application, and no injunction could be granted by any court against it. But things did not just stop at injunction. The bill barred any Indian court to have jurisdiction to entertain any suit concerning the eviction of any person from any Waqf property or demolition of any structure or fixture from any Waqf property.

Luckily, for us encroachers of Allah's land, the hard Congress went away in 2014 and was replaced by the soft Congress. Appeasement continues, if not through this draconian bill, at least in the interim through the 1995 Act.

That the Waqf Act, 1995 is blatantly communal, discriminatory, unconstitutional and draconian is not in contention—one only must read its clauses and sections to realise what a rotten hand Hindus have been dealt with through this act. What adds to the absurdity is the fact that this is now a perpetual motion machine, gobbling up land, property and government largesse with speed and stealth, with every passing day, insatiable in its appetite, as though out to prove Dr Ambedkar and his profound prophecy of Muslims under divine obligation to convert Dar-al-Harb to Dar-al-Islam.[76] It is no longer an arcane endowment that is centuries old; it is an ever-growing mutant, having perfectly adapted to the appeasing and virtue-signalling State.

Hindus who, during the partition, fled what is now Pakistan and came to India, their property was promptly confiscated and either distributed to the Muslim citizenry or taken up by the Government of Pakistan. Not so the case with the Muslims who from India went over to Pakistan. Their property was handed over to Waqf.[77] As a result, the Hindu refugees who came to stay on this land are paying rent that is subject to arbitrary increases. And the injustice continues. Hindus now must beg for Waqf land to celebrate their festival as is what happened recently in Karnataka[78]. However, governments—both the Centre and states—have usurped hundreds of thousands of acres of temple land and are responsible for more than 100,000 temples losing lacs of crores in rental income. There is no such Act for Hindus. There is no such act for Sikhs. There is no such act for Christians. There is no such act even for Muslims in Muslim majority countries like Turkey, Sudan and Egypt. Welcome to the Islamic Republic of India. This is not our future; this is now our present.

4
The RTE Act

All religious schools are equal, but some are less equal than others. This paraphrasing of George Orwell's parodic commandment typifies the thinking of the State when it comes to Hindu-run schools and educational institutions. The Right to Education Act, or the RTE, is the proverbial Moses staff that makes sure this commandment is obeyed. The RTE in itself is a worthy undertaking that states as its preamble: 'An Act to provide for free and compulsory education to all children of the age of 6 to 14 years.'[79] But in terms of discrimination at once casual and concrete, very few acts match up to the RTE. The Act was passed by the Congress-led UPA government back in 2009.[80] Tellingly, it remains in force in the present-day Hindu

Rashtra. Simply put, the RTE continues to destroy Hindu schools and institutions. Perhaps, that is the overarching goal of secularism—to allow the prospering of every other religion, its belief systems, its way of life, its cultural values, its educational methods, its wisdom, its books and scriptures, except Hinduism. And after Hinduism is dead, we will remember it fondly and exhort its glory like we do for every other extinct civilisation and culture. Taxidermy fetish is what it is.

There are numerous provisions under the RTE that selectively apply only to non-Minority schools.[81] For example, you cannot have a capitation fee or screen students you want admitted[82]; the reimbursement of fee by the government is never timely, forcing the school to go under debt, even shut shop.[83] You have to have a government-mandated selection procedure for teachers—one that includes a quota-driven recruitment.[84] There are several building and infrastructural restrictions and requirements that a school must comply with[85]—the list is endless; but the overarching, draconian provision of the

RTE that is proving to be a death knell for privately-run Hindu educational institutions is its order that 25 per cent of the seats must be allotted to children belonging to the economically weaker sections, or EWS,[86] and other disadvantaged groups. This does not apply to minority schools.[87] So the onus of serving the economically weaker section of our society rests only on Hindu-run schools and not on Muslim- or Christian-run institutions.[88]

In 2017, three years after the heralding of the Hindu Rashtra, the National Independent School Alliance, NISA,[89] compiled a list of schools in 12 states that had been asked to shut down by the governments[90] for non-compliance to the RTE's draconian provisions.[91] And as the RTE primarily applies to non-minority schools, one can safely assume these were Hindu-run schools. As many as 7,000 schools in Maharashtra, the bastion of Hindavi Swaraj, had been told to shut down.[92] We need to understand, that the threat of closure does not just intimidate the school, it scares the pupils and the parents too. It has been five years since NISA implored the Centre to relook at the RTE and ease the draconian anti-Hindu strictures. The Hindu Rashtra government is silent.

Now, as the famous lines go:

Jiska koi nahin uska toh khuda hai yaaron,
Ye main nahin kehta, kitabo mein likha hai yaaron.

Which book, you may ask. Well, in a secular nation, we have only one book to fall back on. So let us look at our Constitution. Because if discrimination is cast in stone, we must at least examine the stone. The stone to begin with is Article 30. I now quote verbatim: '1. All minorities, whether based on religion or language, shall have the right to establish and administer educational institutions of their choice. 1A. In making any law providing for the compulsory acquisition of any property of an educational institution established and administered by a minority, referred to in clause 1, the State shall ensure that the amount fixed by or determined under such law for the acquisition of such property is such as would not restrict or abrogate the right guaranteed under that clause. 2. The state shall not, in granting aid to educational institutions, discriminate against any educational institution on the ground that it is under the management of a minority, whether based on religion or language.'[93]

A direct fallout of not only the structure of this Article but its words and composition, is that Muslims in Kashmir, Sikhs in Punjab and Christians in Nagaland are still considered a minority and can run schools that will not be subject to the RTE. In reality, these communities are a majority in the respective states.

Let us now look at Article 28.[94] The central and state governments have discovered enough loopholes in it to violate this article at will to placate their vote bank. The Article states: '1. No religion instruction shall be provided in any educational institution wholly maintained out of State funds. 2. Nothing in clause 1 shall apply to an educational institution which is administered by the State but has been established under any endowment or trust which requires that religious instruction shall be imparted in such institution. 3. No person attending any educational institution recognised by the State or receiving aid out of State funds shall be required to take part in any religious instruction that may be imparted in such institution or to attend any religious worship that may be conducted in such institution or in any premises attached thereto unless such person or, if such person is a minor, his guardian has given his consent thereto Cultural and Educational Rights.

Coupled with this, there is Article 26[95] of our Constitution that ordains 'Freedom to manage religious affairs subject to public order, morality and health', and that 'every religious denomination or any section thereof shall have the right to establish and maintain institutions for religious and charitable purposes; to manage its own affairs in matters of religion; to own and acquire movable and immovable property; and to administer such property in accordance with law.' Read both articles side by side and you realise what you are up against.

Let me now read Clause 5 of Article 15 of our Constitution[96] that was brought in by the UPA government in 2006 as the 93rd Amendment. In Article 15 of the Constitution, after Clause 4, the following clause shall be inserted, namely Clause 5: 'Nothing in this article or in sub-clause (g) of clause (1) of Article 19 shall prevent the State from making any special provision, by law, for the advancement of any socially and educationally backward classes of citizens or for the Scheduled Castes or the Scheduled Tribes in so far as such special provisions relate to their admission to educational institutions including private educational institutions, whether aided or unaided by the State, other than the minority educational institutions referred to in clause 1 of Article 30.'

Now, Article 15 that prohibits discrimination on grounds of religion, race, caste, sex or place of birth already had Clause 4 that allowed States to make special provision for the advancement of any socially and educationally backward classes of citizens or for the Scheduled Castes and the Scheduled Tribes, but it did not exclude minority institutions, and that puts the onus on minorities to also contribute to the society and work towards the upliftment of our socially and educationally backward classes of citizens or for the Scheduled Castes and the Scheduled Tribes. This was unacceptable to the Congress as well as, I must add, the present government because this amendment was passed with the latter's support.[97]

I hope you can see it clearly now that the 93rd Amendment is the staff meant to establish the commandments of Articles 26 and 30, and it is because of the brandishing of this staff that the RTE does not apply to minority-run schools, barring a ubiquitous exception of a ban on corporal punishment that all Indian schools must compulsorily follow.

To summarise the chain of events, the government applies RTE rules selectively to Hindu-run schools, orders them to maintain a 25 per cent EWS quota, does not provide fee reimbursement on time—so much so that back in 2019, as many as 4,000 schools threatened to go on a strike against the delays in fee reimbursement.[98] Unconcerned, governments threaten schools and blackmail them with land occupancy provisions just to escape paying the reimbursement. Schools are forced to hike fees for all pupils in order to escape debt and closure; the fee increase forces Hindu parents to shift their children to other schools. More and more Hindu parents take their children away from Hindu schools and these children are then welcomed by schools run by minorities, and by virtue of the religious obligations and directive principles of the Constitution laid down for the believers, where preaching, proselytisation and conversion are religious duties, these children are inevitably, sometimes subtly, sometimes directly, put under pressure to convert. Meanwhile, Hindu schools are forced to close down. A recent report estimates that the RTE is responsible for the closure of more than 10,000 Hindu-run schools.

A 2017 CAG report noted that the release of funds by the Centre to schools was sometimes delayed by as much as 307 days.[99] Such delays not only lead to outright closure of schools, they also result in abandoning any plans for expansion or upgradation of infrastructure.[100] Ironical because these are the criteria to be fulfilled by schools under the RTE. More importantly, even if the government pays the EWS pupil fee, albeit a year late, the school would still have to shell out for textbooks, uniforms, transport and other ancillary things every school-going child needs, especially when his parents are underpriviledged.[101]

The authority that decides if a school is exempt from the RTE is the National Commission for Minority Education Institutions (NCMEI). Shockingly, this body, although quasi-judicial in its directives, cannot have a Hindu as its member. In fact, BJP leader Ashwini Upadhyay filed a PIL seeking to challenge the NCMEI Act[102] and to allow Hindus to be declared as minorities in the states and Union Territories where they are, well, minorities. This is logical and rational, especially because it has wide-ranging repercussions on the survival of Hindu-run schools in these states and UTs. Hindus are now a minority in Jammu and Kashmir, Mizoram, Arunachal Pradesh, Manipur, Punjab, Nagaland, Meghalaya, Ladakh and Lakshadweep. But one entity has opposed the petition, calling it frivolous. No, that entity was not the Congress or the church or Darul-Uloom. That entity was the central government. The government called his petition 'untenable and misconceived in law'[103] and told the court that the petition was 'not in larger public or national interest'. The Centre backed the same discriminatory National Commission for Minorities Educational Institutions (NCMEI) under whose act only Muslims, Christians, Jains, Sikhs, Buddhists and Parsis are listed as minorities. Following outrage, the present government has only now asked more time from the court to think on the matter.[104] Meanwhile, Hindu-run religious and linguistic schools continue to close under the burden of discriminatory RTE rules.

If there is only one thing more cruel than not allowing Hindu temples to run their own educational institutions without fear of State intervention and control, it is not allowing Hindus to run their own educational institutions without fear of State intervention and control. And if there is only one thing more cruel than the fact that both these cruelties are being subjected on the Hindus, it is that they are being subjected by the Hindus. Belonging to a Hindu government. In a Hindu Rashtra.

5
Legislations that Appease Non-Hindus but Target Hindus

In Hinduism, religion is an offshoot of the way of life, while in Islam, way of life is an offshoot of religion. Because of this distinction, one is amenable to change and reform while in the other, leave alone reform, even changing a punctuation in the holy verses and commandments is expressly forbidden. And herein lies the dichotomy that plagues our State. We will try and reform one religion and its practices but will recoil from reforming the other. We will break and remove the shackles of intolerance from one but will jangle and rattle them with pride for the other. We will constitutionalise reform in one, through legislations, code bills, laws and IPC sections, but will not only stay away from bringing in similar legislations for the other—we will even overturn Supreme Court judgments that aim to bring in limited reform.

Bigamy, for example, is banned under the Indian law, specifically under Section 494 of the IPC, and carries a seven-year jail term,[105] but it is permitted under Section 2 of the Muslim Personal Law (Shariat) Application Act, 1937.[106] This is not to suggest that bigamy should be allowed for Hindus but, rather, to highlight the double standards when it comes to Muslims.

Another case in point is the Prevention of Communal and Targeted Violence (Access to Justice and Reparations) Bill, 2011,[107] or the so-called Communal Violence Bill that was drafted by the Sonia Gandhi constituted and monitored NAC. Fortunately, it never saw the light of day. If it had, it would have been yet another instrument of discrimination against the majority Hindu community. That is because the revised draft changed the definition of the group targeted in communal violence. Henceforth, this 'group' would have meant either a religious or linguistic minority or

Scheduled Castes and Scheduled Tribes. This essentially meant that only minorities and SC/STs could be victims while the perpetrators of communal violence would always be the majority, meaning Hindus. The absurdity of this bill dawned when people realised that Hindus would be branded as perpetrators even when they were the minority, for example in Kashmir, Punjab or Kerala, when SC/STs were subtracted from the Hindu population. Outrageously, this definition was to be used even in cases of sexual assault. When Harsh Mander, one of the NAC members who drafted this ludicrous bill, was asked to explain reasons for such blatant anti-Hindu sentiments, he retorted by saying: 'There is an institutional bias against the minorities that needed to be corrected. In cases of communal violence, the entire criminal justice system has been against minorities. It is to correct this institutional bias that we needed this bill.'[108]

Someone should inform Mr Mander that if at all the entire criminal justice system has been against a community in recent memory, it is against the Kashmiri

Hindus who, 30 years later, are still seeking justice for the rape, murder, ethnic cleansing and genocide perpetrated against their community by Muslims—the so-called minority. But according to this Bill, these crimes could not have happened because the minority could not have committed them. Perhaps, that is why the Supreme Court also refuses to open these cases of atrocities.

The truth is that the State has been blackmailed and browbeaten to such an extent that the so-called liberals, progressives and conscientious feminists outrage on Karvachauth but slither away under their favourite Parthasarathy rock when it comes to giving equal inheritance rights to Muslim women.[109] These feminists will talk of anything but the fact that even courts in our country have begun to ratify the allowance for Muslims to marry on attainment of puberty, violating the most sacrosanct of our Laws, namely the Prohibition of Child Marriage Act. And the high court judge who okayed the marriage of a pubescent Muslim girl is now in the Supreme Court.[110] He was one of the judges who blamed Nupur Sharma for the beheading of the tailor Kanhaiya Lal.

They will claim banning Triple Talaq is an invasion of privacy[111] and an assault on one's freedom of expression.[112] They will not castigate Owaisi or his party for vehemently opposing the removal of leprosy as a ground for divorce[113] because the AIMPLB believes that leprosy—a disease completely curable—is sufficient grounds for divorce. They will not side with Shah Bano. They will abuse anyone who pleads for One India One Law. They will even applaud Mehbooba Mufti who recently called for introducing stoning as a punishment in Kashmir.[114] This is the kind of in-your-face State-sanctioned hypocrisy we are dealing with. Hindus and Hinduism stand no chance. When did they ever?

For centuries, those who have ruled India have sought to bring in reforms only in Hinduism. The British even set up the B.N. Rau Committee in 1941[115] to exclusively codify only Hindu laws. The report of this committee formed the template for the 1951 Hindu Code Bills. The Bill was adopted in

1956[116] and it gives, creditably so, much needed rights to Hindu women, while at the same time, providing equality to the affected parties on a range of civil matters—from succession to marriage, to property rights to guardianship, adoption and maintenance. Any reform is good. It signifies helpful mutations are being accumulated, that the living, breathing organism is adapting to changing times, that it is evolving, and because it is evolving, it will survive. But why should only Hindus and Hinduism be reformed? What about Christians and Christianity? Muslims and Islam?

Everyone is aware of Dr Ambedkar's criticism of Hinduism—as a religion and as a way of life. The Left loses no opportunity to highlight this in books, in debates and documentaries, even in the Parliament. But they remain silent when it comes to highlighting his criticism of Islam. Indeed, Dr Ambedkar was so appalled by selective criticism of Hinduism that he wrote: 'The social evils that characterise the Hindu Society have been well known. But books that expose these evils and call their authors at the bar of the world to answer for their sins, create the unfortunate impression throughout the world that while the Hindus are grovelling in the mud of these social evils and are conservative, the Muslims in India are free from them, and as compared to the Hindus, are a progressive people. That such an impression should prevail is surprising to those who know the Muslim Society in India at close quarters. Take the caste system. Islam speaks of brotherhood. Everybody infers that Islam must be free from caste. But this is not the case. Caste among Muslims has remained. There can thus be no manner of doubt that the Muslim Society in India is afflicted by the same social evils as afflict the Hindu Society. Indeed, the Muslims have all the social evils of the Hindus and something more. That something more is the compulsory system of purdah for Muslim women.'[117]

In 1975, a 62-year-old mother of five, Shah Bano Begum, was thrown out of her house and on to the streets of Indore. She had been married for 43 years to Mohd Ahmed Khan who earned ₹5,000 a month—a princely sum in those days. Three years later, destitute and without a roof over her head, Shah Bano approached the lower courts asking for a maintenance sum of ₹500 a month under Section 125 (1) (a) of the Code of Criminal Procedure. What she got instead was a talaq. In his defence, her husband told the court he had already provided ₹3,000 as Mehr, or dowry, during iddat, a period of waiting that a divorced woman must adhere to before she can remarry. The court sided with the wife and asked the husband to pay a reduced maintenance sum of ₹25 per month. The husband refused, citing the rights given to him under the Muslim Personal Law. The case went to the high court. This time, the husband was directed to pay a maintenance sum of ₹179.20 per month under Section 125. The husband appealed to the Supreme Court.

In a landmark judgment,[118] the Supreme Court dismissed Mohd Ahmed Khan's appeal and directed him to pay maintenance to his ex-wife as laid down by the high court. 'Does the Muslim Personal Law', asked the court, 'impose no obligation upon the husband to provide for the maintenance of his divorced wife? Undoubtedly, the Muslim husband enjoys the privilege of being able to discard his wife whenever he chooses to do so, for reasons good, bad, or indifferent. Indeed, for no reason at all. It is a matter of deep regret that some of the interveners who supported the husband, took up an extreme position by displaying an unwarranted zeal to defeat the right to maintenance of women who are unable to maintain themselves.'

It is not clear who among the bench penned the concluding words of the judgment. What is clear is that whoever they were, are worthy of praise. 'It is also a matter of regret that Article 44 of our Constitution has remained a dead letter. The State shall endeavour to secure for the citizens a uniform civil code throughout the territory of India. A belief seems to have gained ground that it is for the Muslim community to take a lead in the matter of reforms of their personal law. A common Civil Code will help the cause of national integration by removing disparate loyalties to laws which have conflicting ideologies. No community is likely to bell the cat by making gratuitous concessions on this issue. It is the State which is charged with the duty of securing a uniform civil code for the citizens of the country and, unquestionably, it has the legislative competence to do so. A counsel in the case whispered, somewhat audibly, that legislative competence is one thing, the political courage to use that competence is quite another. We understand the difficulties involved in bringing persons of different faiths and persuasions on a common platform, but a beginning has to be made if the Constitution is to have any meaning. Inevitably, the role of the reformer has to be assumed by the courts because it is beyond the endurance of sensitive minds to allow injustice to be suffered when it is so palpable.'[119]

To utter these words takes barely a minute—to write them down perhaps a little longer. But to think them through takes decades of learning and scholarship, and a degree of objectivity that demands detachment. And you know you have failed when it all comes to nought. 'Section 125', the court concluded, 'is truly secular in character. Whether the spouses are Hindus or Muslims, Christians or Parsis, Pagans or Heathens, is wholly irrelevant in the application of these provisions. It would make no difference as to what religion is professed by the neglected wife, child or parent.'

That was the one blunder our Supreme Court committed. Who or what is secular is not to be decided by learned men and women of the highest court in the land. It is, instead, the sole prerogative of the politicians. Only they have the sacrosanct right to deliver this verdict. Exactly a year later, deliver they did. The Rajiv Gandhi-led Congress government, beset with issues of corruption, nepotism and mismanagement, chose the well-travelled route to political expediency and passed The Muslim Women Protection of Rights on Divorce Act 1986.[120] In one fell-swoop, the Supreme Court judgment was overturned. The wording of the 1986 Act conveys to the citizens something the politicians thought had been overlooked, perhaps disregarded—who rules whom. 'Every application by a divorced woman under Section 125 pending before a Magistrate shall be disposed of by such Magistrate in accordance with the provisions of this Act.' Henceforth, the husband was to pay the ex-wife maintenance only during the iddat period. The liability beyond the iddat rested not on the husband but on those relatives who would receive the ex-wife's property upon her death, failing which, the Waqf Board was to take responsibility.

Shah Bano was on the streets again and India was back to being secular.

6

Judiciary that Almost Exclusively Tries to Reform Hinduism

On 1 July 2022, the Supreme Court refused to entertain a plea to club multiple FIRs against Nupur Sharma for merely quoting what is derived from the revered Islamic scriptures Sahih al-Bukhari 5134; Book 67, Hadith 70,[121] and Sunan an-Nasa'i 3378; Vol. 4, Book 26, Hadith 3380.[122] The court could have left it at that and dismissed the case and the judges broken for lunch, but they did not.[123] It is not for me to judge the judges, but let me quote them and then leave it for you to decide whether their remarks against a helpless, victimised, shunned, discarded, hunted young Hindu woman were not bolstered by decades of institutional vilification, ridicule and discrimination against Hindus. Things do not happen in isolation; they build upon existing edifices, brick by punishing brick.

'You have ignited the whole country and you have the cheek and courage to come to the court to ask for discretionary relief?' cried the judges. 'You are singlehandedly responsible for the burnings in the country. Your statement is responsible for the unfortunate killing in Udaipur [where a Hindu tailor was beheaded on camera for supporting Nupur Sharma]. Are you facing a security threat, or have you become a threat to the security of the nation? You possess a loose tongue and keep on making irresponsible statements. You should apologise to the whole country for your remarks made either for cheap publicity, political agenda, or some nefarious activities. Your petition shows your obstinate character and your arrogance that you think that the Magistrate Courts are too small for you. Sometimes power goes to your head and people think they have a backup, and they can make any kind of statement and go scot-free. You went on a channel and made irresponsible statements without even an inkling of the ramifications and serious consequences that how seriously it will disturb the fabric of the society.'

That the legislature discriminates against Hindus is not news—I have provided enough examples. Plenty more exist of minority appeasement at the cost of the majority, but what is to be done when the judiciary singles out the Hindus? What is the recourse then? What is the recourse when you find that the fine lady who stands atop our temples of justice belligerent, when you find her sword that is pointing to the skies blunted and her blindfold perforated, when you find her scales rusted? What is the recourse? There is none. Because while the Supreme Court decides to remove discrimination from Islam, it is stopped from doing so by the Parliament. When it decides to remove perceived discrimination from Hinduism, it is encouraged to do so by the Parliament.

I talk here of the infamous 2018 Sabarimala verdict of the Supreme Court that went against the temple and its centuries-old tradition dictated to its keepers by the celibate deity himself. Recall the iconic statement of the dissenting judge in the original Sabarimala Judgment: 'Notions of rationality cannot be invoked in matters of religion.'[124] Truer words were never spoken. Is it up to the Supreme Court to counsel and inform billions of believers that the Holy Ganges could not have emanated from the trusses of Lord Shiva, or that Prophet Mohammed could not have travelled to heaven on a winged horse, or that Jesus Christ could not have walked on water or turned water to wine? Yes, the courts do have a role to play in intervening and preventing oppressive and hurtful religious practices, but then again, what is hurtful to you or me may not be hurtful to the believer. For example, I believe that stipulating a dress code is oppressive, but can the Supreme Court ban it? If it does, it would be violating the direct commandments of Allah as revealed in the Holy Quran (24:31; 33:59; 7:26). Would that be acceptable to Muslims as well as to all those liberals and feminists who cheered the Sabarimala verdict that vetoed the discrimination? Was it discrimination or perceived discrimination, to begin with? After all, there are many Hindu temples where men are barred entry,[125] such as the Kamakhya Temple, Brahmaji Temple, Kumari Amman Temple, Attukal Bhagavathy Temple and Mata Temple; and there are many Hindu temples, including many Lord Ayyappa Temples, where menstruating women are allowed entry.[126] It is only in this particular Lord Ayyappa shrine that, because of the vow of the deity to remain celibate, menstruating women in a particular age bracket are not allowed to enter. As for menstruating women, it is expressly forbidden for them to touch the Quran, recite a complete verse, enter a mosque, do salat, perform tawaf, fast or have sex (56:79, 2:222; Tirmidhi 315 and Hadith-i Sharif). So, are we now going to redact these verses?

There exists a fundamental contradiction between Articles 21 [right to life, dignity and liberty] and 25 [right to practise any religion] of our Constitution. If one follows or respects one, it is impossible to follow or respect the other. This is because there are tens of thousands of religious commandments, directives, decrees that directly contradict Article 21. If you are a true Catholic woman, you cannot be ordained as a priest. If you are a true Muslim woman, you cannot sing, dance, play sports, drink, fornicate, be a homosexual, wear what you want or be an apostate. A progressive, secular State that, correctly, removes discriminatory practices from the Hindu religion but cowers behind a lamppost like a wet cat when it comes to removing discriminatory practices from other religions is not a progressive, secular State—it is a scared State. The truth is that one would have to be an atheist to always override Article 25 and support Article 21. I, being a Darwinian atheist, am fine with this. But are you, are the judges, are the politicians, are millions of my countrymen and women? *That* is the question. And till the time you answer it, why reform and tinker and restructure and amend only Hinduism while leaving other religions alone? Why bring in legislations and laws and judgments exclusively for Hindus and Hinduism?

In 2019, the Tripura High Court banned animal sacrifice even though Hindus argued that this practice was a centuries-old tantric tradition of worshipping the 10 Mahavidyas, namely Kali, Tara, Tripura Sundari, Bhuvaneshvari, Bhairavi, Chhinnamasta, Dhumavati, Bagalamukhi, Matangi and Kamala. What the Hindus pleaded was also in keeping with the famous 1954 Shirur Mutt Judgment[127] that established the sanctity of an essential religious practice. But the judges would hear none of it. 'No person including the State shall be allowed to sacrifice any animal or bird within the precincts of any temple within the State of Tripura,' they roared.[128] In 2014, the judges of Himachal Pradesh High Court had similarly banned the 600-year-old tradition of animal sacrifice during Kullu Dussehra.[129] In 2017, the quasi-judicial NGT ordered a ban on the tolling of bells and the chanting of shlokas by devotees at Amarnath.[130] Praise the lord, they simultaneously did not allow the delivery of Azaan through a loudspeaker there. Or perhaps, they indeed did but the vagaries of the State have meant the order is yet to reach Bholenath's abode.

The question to be asked is, why should only the religious Hindu be prevented from conducting animal sacrifice? If the State is against animal sacrifice, and laudably so, then should not it be against all animal sacrifices conducted in the name of religion? But is that the case? If the hon'ble courts object to the taking of the life of an animal through a religious ritual, do they have the guts to ban halal? Every single day, more than a billion Muslims eat meat after this religious ritual has been performed. In fact, it is an essential requirement. The Dhabihah—or the prescribed ritual slaughter—must be staged. The incision must be precise and deep that cuts the carotid artery and the trachea. The blood must be drained completely, this while the animal is still alive. The head of the animal must be aligned to the Kaaba. And it is essential that *Bismillah-e-Rahman-e-Rahim* be uttered. Furthermore, only a Muslim can perform the slaughter. So according to the hon'ble judges, this is not a ritual? In fact, this ritualistic practice has been deemed so cruel in many European countries that it is mandatory to stun the animal before performing halal.[131] But do our judges have the courage to shun selectivity when it comes to animal rights?

Hindu festivals and celebrations and sporting events are easy target, be it Jallikattu or Kambala or Nagapanchami, or even kite flying during Makar Sankranti, or believe it or not, restricting the height of the dahi handi during the Janmashtami festival. The judges have capped the human pyramid height to twenty feet, saying anything above would inflict harm to the participating humans. 'We only know of Krishna stealing butter; did he also indulge in acrobatics while stealing it?' mocked the judges.[132]

I want to ask the judges—what happens to all their mockery and colourful retorts when it comes to Moharram, where tens of thousands of Muslims openly inflict serious bodily harm to themselves and to others, with whips laced with steel claws that stab deep into the devotee's flesh amid chants of *Ya Abbas, Ya Abbas*. Is that not inflicting harm? But does our State or its arms have the guts to ban this ritual during Moharram?

It is the same with banning crackers during Diwali but allowing millions of tons of stubble to be burnt during the same month, or millions of trees to be cut during Christmas, or allowing fireworks during new year celebrations, because apparently, only Diwali is increasing the carbon footprint and contributing to pollution—the rest are purifying the environment. And for those who blame Diwali for the state of Delhi air every year, here is some perspective: An area of 17,900 sq km, or 12 times the size of Delhi, is on fire, continuously, for weeks on end, right next to Delhi. Thirty-five million tonnes of stubble are burnt right under the noses of our judges.[133]

Honestly, I am now convinced—the only way stubble burning can be banned is if we call it Parali Dahan, a Hindu festival wherein according to the Atharva Veda, lord Vishnu burnt demon king Paralisura when he enslaved Maruts and storm king Rudra. Only then will it be banned.

Stubble-burning releases 149 million tons of carbon-dioxide,[134] which is 55 per cent of all Indian transport carbon-dioxide emission.[135] The financial burden of treating the resulting respiratory diseases alone is 154 times more than the cost of the machines needed for stubble extraction.[136] But if our politicians and judges thought like this, we would be a developed nation.

And with our courts acting the way they are towards Hindus and their rituals, can the State be far behind? Dharmapuram Adheenam's Pattina Pravesam, the ancient Hindu ritual of carrying the priest, has now been banned,[137] and that too by invoking clauses of forced labour. You mean to tell me the devotees are being forced to carry the pontiff they revere? What next? I will tell you what next. There will soon come a time when the State will ban the pulling of the lord Jagannath on the pretext of forced labour.

But there will never come a time when the State bans Sedia Gestatoria, the tradition of carrying a Christian priest. There will never come a time when the State bans the hoisting of the bulky tazia on dozens of tired exhausted shoulders during Moharram. There will never come a time when the State bans the tradition of carrying a heavy wooden cross on Easter parade. There will never come a time when the State bans male genital circumcision, a religion-ordained act of cruelty that is banned in many European countries.[138]

This selectivism against only Hindu festivals and religious practices will soon result in a scenario where the Hindus begin to dislike their own traditions. From there, the road to self-loathing is but a few yards away, and we know where that road leads to—forsaking Hinduism itself and accepting another religion. As if on cue, the courts have recently opined that non-Hindus cannot be barred by temples into setting up their shops on temple premises.[139] 'We cannot allow this,' thundered the bench. So let me get this straight. A man whose religion orders him to viscerally hate the Hindu, commands him to convert this infidel, and if he cannot, then kill him at an opportune moment; a man whose religion tells him no one has the right to be worshipped but Allah 40:62; that those who deny the Quran their necks will be shackled 40:70; that polytheists or Hindus are the worst of creatures 98:6; that fight against those who do not believe in Allah and who do not adopt Islam, fight them until they give the jizya while they are humbled 9:29; that do not marry polytheist women unless they believe in Islam 2:221; that those who disbelieve in our verses we will drive them into a Fire 4:56; that do not take disbelievers as friends unless they convert and kill them if they refuse 4:89— the court orders the Hindu temple to give this man the temple's own land to set up a shop in. Is there a finer example of how entrenched snubbing of Hindu interests has become?

There is no other way of saying this: The camel has begun to sneak into the tent. An open sky awaits.

7
Celebrating Those Who Killed and Converted Millions of Hindus

To visit Nalanda, the ancient place of learning and arguably India's greatest cultural heritage, one needs to board a train from Delhi and get down 50 miles from Patna at a place called Bakhtiyarpur. From Bakhtiyarpur, it is a brief and pleasant journey to Nalanda, and when you reach this hallowed place, when you stroll about its manicured lawns and thin brick facades and ruins, you will get to know how this magnificent temple of knowledge and wisdom was charred to the ground by a barbarian; how thousands of scholars perished in the fires that burnt for months; how millions of books were reduced to cinders; how a civilisation the world envied and admired as a Vishwaguru was lost forever; and, that, the barbarian who executed this vicious act was none other than Bakhtiyar. Yes. Bakhtiyar. And we have named not only a railway station but also a city in his honour.[140] Our destruction that even Bakhtiyar could not manage in his lifetime is now complete.

A 1,000 years later, that we have honoured this barbarian is not hurtful enough; what hurts most is that because we are so unsatisfied and unsatiated with this hideous self-flagellation, we have endeavoured to descend a step further into the dungeons of distorted history and peddled the narrative that Bakhtiyar did not even destroy or set fire to Nalanda. Instead, we have blamed a couple of Hindu beggars[141] for burning down the great city of Nalanda. That's right—not an invader and his army of tens of thousands but, rather, two gawky little Hindu beggars were responsible for destroying the greatest ancient university there ever was.

I do not have the inclination to narrate to you in detail the figments of Leftist historian D.N. Jha's mind and its imaginings;

the fact that he never quoted a primary source for his assertion; the fact that the first English translation of Jha's source *Pag Sam Jon Zang*[142] was carried out as late as a 100 years ago; the fact that it never even mentions the two Hindu beggars—but the fact remains, that Jha has won this war of narratives. Bakhtiyar lives.

'For the sake of Islam, I became a wanderer, I battled infidels and the Hindus, I was determined to become a martyr; Thanks be to Allah I became a Ghazi!'[143]—This is a direct quote of Babur, from *Baburnama*. There is a Babur Road in Central Delhi, barely a mile from the prime minister's residence. Babur lives.

'Hindu gods and their idols are as dirty as they are ugly and horrible to look at, and witnessing the destruction of temple idols gives me so much joy.'[144] The man who said this was also the chief proponent of the Goa inquisition, that led to the conversion, torture and murder of thousands of Hindus.[144] His name was St Francis Xavier. Every year, millions of Indians, including our Hindu nationalist

Prime Minister Narendra Modi, venerate him. St Francis Xavier lives.

Sikandar Shah Miri (1389–1413), who commissioned Jamia Masjid and is still eulogised in Kashmir, collected 3 *khirwars*, or 210 kilogrammes, of sacred thread from Kashmiri Hindus before he burnt them.[145] A single sacred thread weighs 7 grams. I shall leave it to the mathematicians among you to calculate the sheer scale of the genocide. Sikandar Shah Miri lives.

'I will raze these Anasagar Hindu temples to the ground. I have come to India to fight the holy war against the infidels.'[146] The man who said this was Khwaja Moinuddin Chishti, the Hanafi Sufi saint who fought alongside the demonic Muhammed Ghauri and unsparingly converted Hindus. Every year, millions of Indians, including our Hindu nationalist Prime Minister Narendra Modi offer a *chadar* at his Mazar and venerate him. Moinuddin Chishti lives.

We know more about the Mughals than about Shivaji, Rana Pratap and Prithviraj Chauhan. Why? Because history that is written by the victors is peddled by the vanquished. And we have been vanquished. This is a country where people still go and pray at the grave of Aurangzeb who beheaded Guru Tegh Bahadur, decapitated Sambhaji Maharaj, demolished Kashi Vishwanath and murdered 4.6 million Hindus.[147] This is a country where Guru Arjan Dev was forced to sit on a hot plate and literally cooked alive by the Mughal Emperor Jahangir and what do we do? We immortalise Jahangir in our films as the affable feather-toying romantic Salim. This is a country where a celebrated historian Ramchandra Guha did not want Delhi roads to be named after Chhatrapati Shivaji—the man who birthed an empire stretching from Peshawar to Plassey—because, in Guha's words, he was a 'little-known regional figure and a feudal lord who endorsed caste hierarchies'.[148] This is a country where we eulogise the invaders, who, over many centuries, perpetrated the largest genocide in human history and murdered 80 million of us, a figure arrived at authoritatively by Historians K.S. Lal and Will Durant.[149] This is a country where Kareena Kapoor and

Saif Ali Khan take pride in naming their son Taimur; where Akhilesh Yadav takes pride in having the nickname Tipu.

Our history has been written by those who hated Hindus, Hinduism and Hindustan. Our history *is* being written by those who hate Hindus, Hinduism and Hindustan. There are hundreds of examples but just one would suffice. Tipu Sultan. Read his Manifesto, written in his own words.[150] It is a terrifying proclamation calling for all Muslims to come together to wage Jihad. Annihilation of the infidels is a sacred duty, he writes. The Hindus of Koorg suffered a particularly brutal onslaught. Murders, tortures, forced conversions. Even dead Hindus were converted. Even dead Hindus! Tipu destroyed more than 800 temples, 27 churches, captured 60,000 Christians, converted 30,000 and killed thousands;[151] chroniclers Lewis Rice[152] and R.D. Palsokar believe the figure could be as high as 8,000 temples.[153] Descendants of Mandyam Iyengars do not celebrate Diwali till this day.[154] Ever wondered why? Tipu butchered them on this day. Read Bartolomeo's personal account of Tipu Sultan's butchery in Calicut. Men, women and children were paraded naked and trampled by elephants. And yet, we call Tipu a 'Symbol of Communal Harmony'. We cheer when the statue of the evil racist king Leopold is demolished in Belgium, but we celebrate Tipu Jayanti. Because tyrants who murder Hindus are not tyrants but heroes? Praising Tipu is like praising King Leopold for building roads and ports in Congo, balancing out ivory and rubber trade and a million murders. There is no difference between Tipu Sultan apologists and Holocaust deniers. And yet they exist, in their millions.

In years to come, I am sure Yakub Memon's grave would become as popular a worshipping place as Aurangzeb's is today, visited and prayed at by politicians and film stars. The same Aurangzeb, who was Baghdadi 350 years before ISIS. The genocide he perpetrated claimed 4.6 million Hindu lives. If an incident could muster a million spine-chilling imaginings, it would be that of the one in 1675 under broad daylight in Chandni Chowk where Guru Tegh Bahadur was beheaded on the orders of Aurangzeb. And yet, we have cities and roads named after him—we have his tomb consecrated and turned into a memorial. Seventy-five years have gone, but we still have not got independence from brainwashing and servitude. And that is why, in years to come, Yakub Memon would be celebrated just like Aurangzeb is. After all, tens of thousands attended his funeral, tears flowing down their cheeks. People will come and pray at his grave, seek his blessings.

From the Aryans to Aurangzeb, from St Xavier to Shivaji, our historians have chosen what to hide, what to invent and what to disclose. The singular reason for this is the craving for patronage—of an ideology, a government, an ecosystem or a clique. Villains are made into heroes and heroes into villains. We like it this way. Our historical figures are to be worshipped; they are to be made into Gods, into Atlases who carry the weight of our ideologies and our biases on the nape of their necks. History as myth; myth as history. It conforms to what we really are—unsure of our present and fearful of our future. Fear and trembling, that is what this is, and the whole nation chugs along on this dead yet simmering coal. A journey to nowhere—slow, halting and tiring—until you realise what the grand plan always is—to appropriate invaders and to forget our own.

How else do we explain appropriating foreign destructive ideologies and their proponents like Karl Marx, Mao, Che? Can you now appreciate how reading and imbibing a particular history can weaken a nation? Because when you eulogise monsters like Che, Mao and Polpot, you also decide to walk on their paths—you weaken the nation. Look at what the communists did to Bengal. Look at what they did to anything they have touched. And they still venerate Stalin and Mao. Mao, who killed 63 million of his own people. And if you think I am talking abstract and philosophical gibberish, recall who wanted to scuttle the Indo-US nuclear deal, who was against the green revolution, against river linking, against dams, recall who forbade the setting up of blood donation camps during the 1962 war with China, recall who hailed the Tiananmen Square massacre, recall who was against liberalisation. They are still very much among us, in our society, in our committees, in our universities, in our parliament. The more we are ignorant of our history, the more we are taught it wrongly, the more we clear the path for them to return to power.

History, for us, is either to be hidden or invented. We tell and retell what we like of it, and of what we do not, we scrunch it up and slip it under the mattress. For the victors, a quill to write history with; for the vanquished, the burden to peddle it. But we forget: History is not Homeopathy —it does not work as a placebo when diluted, it simply disappears. Every city a Hindu lives in, every school he attends, every university he goes to, every road he walks on, he cannot escape being confronted by his cruel past, that raped, mutilated, murdered and converted him; he cannot escape being humiliated by it, pummelled again by it, by the force of history, condensed and packed into a punch that lands and lands, and keeps on landing, until the Hindu is lying face down on the canvas, blood-laced spit bubbling from his lips. This is a Hindu Rashtra, they say. I ask them: Is there a Hitler Road in Tel Aviv?

8
Places of Worship Act, 1991

History that is written by the victors, I had remarked earlier, is peddled by the vanquished, and as far as I am concerned, one of the most barbaric legislations ever peddled in India is the 1991 Places of Worship Act.[155] But in 2019, the virtue-signalling Supreme Court in its Ayodhya Judgment[156] wilfully ratified this Act that obligates maintaining all religious places, except Ram Janambhoomi, as they were on 15 August 1947—a 75-year-old date in an 8,000-year-old civilisation. Historical injustice of Kashi or Mathura can now never be addressed unless the Parliament overrides not only this barbaric act but also the Supreme Court's perfidious ratification of it.

A legal recourse to correct historical injustices cannot be denied in a democracy.

And this is not a Hindu issue. I, as a Darwinian atheist, demand the abrogation of the Places of Worship Act. If a mosque had been demolished by a Hindu king and a temple built on it, I, a kaffir, and an atheist for whom Islam sanctions death penalty, would have fought for the right of Muslims to legally get back their mosque. History is but a collection of images—pregnant, expecting, screaming; and if an image could deliver a million words, it would be that of the Nandi waiting patiently for 400 years for his lord to emerge. Will he have to wait for another 400 years?

Nations weaken not because of their past, but rather, by how they are taught it. For 70 years, we have been taught to celebrate the Mathura Idgah and the Gyanwapi Mosque as monuments to Hindu–Muslim unity and not as what they really are, cruel historical injustices. Because for 70 years, we have been taught to forget cruel historical injustices. From Somnath to Kashi Vishwanath, Babarpur to Bakhtiarpur, from Allahabad to Aurangabad, these injustices have deliberately been made visible, as though to lionise the debasement, celebrate the humiliation. And the irony is that the same people who have taught us this, drilled this self-loathing in us—these same people want others to fight historical injustices around the world. They condemn barbarians of the West hitherto worshipped like the Confederacy generals, Rhodes, Churchill, Pizarro, Murray, Colston, Leopold. They celebrate their roads and buildings being renamed, their statues being brought down illegally,[157] but here, in India, this same set eulogises barbarians like Tipu, Aurangzeb, Babur, Khilji. They celebrate the destruction of Kashi, Mathura, Ayodhya, Martand. It is a heady mix of hatred for Hinduism and love for Jihadism, hatred for India and love for its break up.

To show you the extent of the conceit, here is a passage from the 2019 Ayodhya Judgment where the honourable judges exult and wilfully ratify this Act. To recreate the imagery of what those who sat that sultry day in the court and heard these words uttered by the highest court in the land, I will provide, after every sentence, phonetic equivalents of whips lashing one's back in a self-flagellating orgy of destruction and humiliation. 'The Places of Worship Act imposes a bar on the institution of fresh suits or legal proceedings with the only exception, other than Babri Masjid–Ram Janambhoomi case, being appeals or proceedings pending at the commencement of the law on the ground that conversion of a place of worship had taken place after 15 August 1947.' *Whoosh, thwack*! 'The Places of Worship Act is thus a legislative intervention which preserves non-retrogression as an essential feature of our secular values being as it is intrinsically related to the obligations of a secular state.' *Wallop, smack*! 'It reflects the commitment of India to the equality of all religions.' *Whizz, thump*! 'Above all, the Places of Worship Act is an affirmation of the solemn duty which was cast upon the State to preserve and protect the equality of all faiths as an essential constitutional value, a norm which has the status of being a basic feature of the Constitution.' *Whack, slap*! 'There is a purpose underlying the enactment of the Places of Worship Act and which is that the law speaks to our history and to the future of the nation.'

Are you lacerated enough? Is the wound satisfyingly deep? This law speaks to our history and to the future of the nation? No. This law airbrushes our history and destroys our future.

Oil the cat-o-nine tales of your whip, run them lovingly through the hollow of your palm, prepare your singed back for another assault, for the Supreme Court was not done yet. It then gloats and goes on to underline what the home minister said while tabling this barbaric act. The purpose of enacting the law was explained by the Union Minister of Home Affairs on the floor of the Lok Sabha on 10 September 1991—'We see this Bill as a measure to provide and develop our glorious traditions of love, peace and harmony. These traditions are part of a cultural heritage of which every Indian is justifiably proud. Tolerance for all faiths has characterised our great civilisation since time immemorial.'

Never forget that these politicians and these judges enacted this draconian Act to preserve the characteristic of our civilisation. They spoke and acted as though they, and not us, understand what a civilisation is—and because they are the keepers of its characteristics, they must act for us, no matter how unjust or undemocratic the consequences of their actions might be. So I ask—what is civilisation? How do you define it? Is it an idea to be thrust upon the subjects so they carry it forward; is it the placement of forks on the left and spoons on the right of resplendent crockery; is it sartorial splendour; is it words uttered or written; is it science; is it ease of living; is it consumption; is it money? Many of the worst tyrants, who killed millions, wiped off entire races, even continents, have been poets, artists, proponents of science; but would you call their endowments as promoting or harbouring a civilisation? To me, the mark of civilisation is this unquenchable thirst of man to demand justice for his ancestors; to correct a historical wrong. For that exemplifies a continuity; an idea, a memory that can never be erased; that is worth fighting for and preserving. It makes justice greater than the sum of its parts. And that is why civilisations are not fleeting like empires. To demand justice for a people who are dead for hundreds of years, it is almost as though you can feel their pain, their suffering, their destruction, that has transcended the limits of body and time. And that is why history is a medicine; why catharsis is a cure. And when I see the Ram Janambhoomi being reclaimed, I see it as a catharsis, as a deliverance of justice to my ancestors who were wronged. I do not know what shape the temple would take; I do not know when it would ultimately come up; in a way, being an atheist, these issues are not of importance to me. But I know for a fact, that the deliverance has come. It is confounding to me because I am but a bunch of cells, here today gone tomorrow; but till the time I am alive, this concept of striving to correct a historical justice is vital; it defines who I am, what civilisation I am a part of. That erasing my genes cannot erase my civilisation.

The concept of justice is like memory. It keeps getting passed on until realised.

And to those who now call this nation a Hindu Rashtra, run by religious zealots and fascists, to those I ask: In which theocratic state would religious zealots wait for half a millennium and even then, 1 billion people strong, leave it to 5 people to decide the fate of their demand, their yearning, the consecration of their soul itself? This is what makes me proud, that India through the delivery and acceptance of the Ayodhya Judgment, has written her history with the grammar of justice, not anarchy. This moment throws up a milieu of connected philosophical conundrums, one of them being: Should a judge be the product of the society, or should a society be the product of the judge? As I said, 5 judges took the call; the alternative was for 1 billion Hindus to take it. Academy prevailed over anarchy and I am proud that it did.

On the Babri Masjid–Ram Janambhoomi issue, one must read the Supreme Court and the Allahabad High Court judgments to really understand why quack Leftist historians spread so many lies that the courts had to step in to blast them for their perfidy and mediocrity. They said the 50 excavated temple pillars were placed there; they said the Vishnu Hari inscription was stolen from the Lucknow Museum and brought there; they said there was a Buddhist shrine there, there was a Jain shrine there, there was a mosque there, but that there was no Hindu temple underneath the dome. Ultimately, all their lies came to nothing, as the judges rejected all their claims and accepted that there indeed was a Hindu temple underneath the dome and that the dome did not have its foundations but was raised on existing walls. This is what the court said about one Professor Suvira Jaiswal: 'She claims that the disputed building was constructed in the sixteenth century by Babar at Ayodhya called Babri mosque and this statement she is making as a historian, but simultaneously on page 105 she said that she has not read anything about Babri mosque and did not study thoroughly and, therefore, cannot say as to when Babri mosque came into existence.'[158] Historian after quack Historian was exposed. Here is R.C. Thakran: 'In newspapers, I have read

Babur had built a mosque in Ayodhya. As a historian, I consider newspapers to be a source of knowledge. I myself never did any excavation in any field.'[159] Here is the court on the expert Professor Sushil Srivastava. 'Though the witness has been produced as expert historian, but on page 222, he admits that he had very little knowledge of history.'[160]

There is no other way of putting it—the only bulwarks for justice are science and evidence. I take you back to the story of the Turin shroud that for 2,000 years was believed to have been used for wrapping the body of Jesus Christ after crucifixion. Until, in 1989, when scientists proved through carbon-dating that it was only 600 years old.[161] Science teaches us to not fear our past. Law teaches us those nations that fear their past, fear their future. The Places of Worship Act teaches us not only to fear our past but also to fear our future.

That's why I say, in the matter of Ayodhya or Kashi or Mathura, the Hindus must be thanked for pleading before the court to seek justice. If the holiest shrine of some other religion was demolished and people of other faith washed their dirty feet all around the sacred relic, this country would have witnessed a civil war. This atheist owes a debt of gratitude to a billion Hindus who are writing their history with the grammar of justice, not anarchy. Especially because it is beyond any doubt that Aurangzeb ordered the demolition of the Kashi Vishwanath Temple and ordered that the Gyanwapi mosque be built over it. Only those who have read their history from WhatsApp university believe otherwise. It is written in most authentic biography of Aurangzeb, *Masir-e-Alamgiri*, that in 1669, on orders of Aurangzeb, the Kashi Vishwanath Temple was demolished. And then, one year later, he ordered the demolition of the temple at Mathura and had the idols brought to Agra to be scattered under the steps of the Begam Sahab Mosque so that they would be trodden on. The Farman is also archived in Bikaner Archives.[162] And here is Sir Jadunath Sarkar's translation of *Masir-e-Alamgiri*—'Aurangzeb, eager to establish Islam, issued orders to the governors of all provinces to demolish the schools and temples of the infidels and with the utmost urgency put down the teachings and the public practice of the religion of these misbelievers.'[163] And yet, there are those who deny the Hindus their legitimate right to correct historical injustice. And principal among them are our legislature and the judiciary, through the 1991 Places of Worship Act. And that is also why I profoundly disagree with the RSS Chief Dr Mohan Bhagwat when he says: 'Why look for shivling in every mosque?'[164] I find his statement flippant, frivolous and an insult to all those who seek to legally correct historical injustices.

You may say that as a Darwinian atheist I have no legitimate right to intervene. But I assert that this is not a Hindu issue. Or a religious issue. Looking for a shivling, one shivling or ten or ten thousand, reclaiming demolished, destroyed places of worship, correcting historical injustices, is an Indian issue. It is a civilisational issue. The historian Shri Sitaram Goel meticulously tabulated 1862 mosques that are built upon demolished temples.[165] According to J. Sai Deepak[166] and

Vikram Sampath, this number is as high as 40,000.[167] And that is why we need to look for each and every shivling, wherever it is, hidden or exposed, underground or over it. We owe it to our ancestors. We owe it to justice itself. Because as I said, the concept of justice is like memory. It keeps getting passed on until realised. Why shouldn't Nandi be washed of the sins the tyrants committed on him and his lord's abode?

> *His legs buckled, his eyes wet*
> *Carved in stone, but heart beset*
> *He sat outside with perked up ears*
> *Waiting patiently for 400 years*
> *He saw the monster and his hordes*
> *Charge his lord with rusted swords*
> *He saw them wash, he saw them spit*
> *In those waters of the pit*
> *He heard their cries, he heard their call*
> *He lived through it, he saw it all*
> *But not a whisper, not a groan*
> *Life he knew was but on loan*
> *And then, after centuries of pain*
> *When his moment of joy came*
> *He saw them claim*
> *It was just a fountain.*

Epilogue

These, then, are the eight reasons why Hindus in this so-called Hindu Rashtra are not just second-class but, rather, eighth-class citizens. I dare say most Hindus are not even aware of this legislative, judicial and Constitutional apartheid. I confess, I myself was not until a few months ago. Because over these past nine years, not a day has gone by when the Left—that holds a monopoly on the media narrative in India—principally through academic inbreeding and entrenched entitlement and a collectivised belief, that come what may, the system will protect them—not a day has gone by when the Left has not indulged in wanton propaganda, selectivism, scaremongering, Hinduphobia, shameless hypocrisy and the institutionalisation of false equivalence. From spreading misinformation and fake news to pillorying institutions like the

Election Commission and the Armed Forces, nothing was left to chance. The intellectuals have turned into pretenders.

And the pretenders have turned into potters. They have made sure the soft clay that gets baked ultimately into wisdom and sagacity is now the clay of untold misery and mediocrity. But it was not always like that—no it was not.

The clay is special. It is the same clay that suckled the glorious Vedas that fed us, whose richness reflected silently the greatness of its people; whose texture echoed unity in diversity, whose fragrance recalled Bankim and Bharati and Vivekananda and Ambedkar and C.V. Raman, whose blood birthed Shivaji and Subhas Chandra Bose and the great revolutionaries. It is the same clay. It is that same clay that trundles down our mountains and is washed over by the sin-obliterating waters of our holy rivers, and while they wait to receive that same clay, receive it in their trembling hands at Gangasagar before it is lost forever in the vast oceans of apathy, while they wait, we have work to do, to make sure they receive this clay and then shape it into a new India, a great India where a billion Hindus would simply be allowed to live and exist without being discriminated against. They do not ask for much; they never have, and as to the question whether they never will, I leave that on them. As the great Navajo saying goes, you cannot wake a person pretending to be asleep.

Afterword

By the time one finishes reading this meticulously referenced and eloquently well-written book, one is filled with a deep sense of horror, rage and pathos—horror and rage for living as blissfully unaware Hindus in a wonderland, unilaterally bearing the cross of secularism on our shoulders and at our peril; and pathos, as no succour seems to be in sight even from supposed pro-Hindu dispensations. Dr Anand Ranganathan, amongst the numerous hats that he effortlessly wears, is a prolific writer and a conscientious thinker, who never shies away from calling a spade a bloody shovel. *Hindus in Hindu Rashtra* is a distillation of everything that he has been articulating so courageously from numerous platforms since the last several years. Based on an extensive research of various sources on the multiple themes that he addresses in this book, Dr Ranganathan has painted for us a gloomy picture of the present and the future of Hindus in the only country in the world where they have numerical strength of some consequence.

From the Gandhian and Nehruvian era mala fide fantasies to the current one of intense polarisation and vote-bank politics, the interests of the Hindu have always been relegated to the last priority. She is perennially called upon to eschew her identity and consciousness in the larger interests of 'secularism', even as every other community has the freedom to flaunt it, and even exploit it for political, community and electoral benefits. This book elucidates with detailed facts and documentation about how the Hindu community's rights have been trampled upon in various realms—the freedom to control or reclaim its places of worship, rejuvenate its education centres, to look at its own past and its heroes and villains, in blatantly unfair legislations, in judicial remedies, in the protection of its life, property and liberty—in short, its very existence.

In his characteristic blunt, unswerving, and hard-hitting style, Dr Ranganathan has rightly built a case for what he terms as state-enabled apartheid in a country that is ironically being pilloried worldwide as being on the cusp of a violent, morbid Hindu Rashtra, gobbling up all its minorities in a calculated genocide. This work illustrates authoritatively that the boot is actually on the other foot. If, even after reading a scholarly and evocative work like this—a small masterpiece in its own right—the Hindus and the Governments of this country do not wake up to take control and address these issues, the fate of the community will sadly be akin to that of lambs being quietly led to their own slaughter.

Dr Vikram Sampath
Historian, Fellow of the Royal Historical Society

Notes and References

1. http://www.gandhiashramsevagram.org/gandhi-literature/mahatma-gandhi-collected-works-volume-94.pdf
2. http://www.gandhiashramsevagram.org/gandhi-literature/mahatma-gandhi-collected-works-volume-26.pdf
3. http://www.gandhiashramsevagram.org/gandhi-literature/mahatma-gandhi-collected-works-volume-39.pdf
4. https://economictimes.indiatimes.com/news/politics-and-nation/minorities-must-have-first-claim-on-resources-pm/articleshow/754218.cms?from=mdr
5. https://www.youtube.com/watch?v=TMuNWgh7OFE
6. https://www.pradhanmantriyojana.co.in/shaadi-shadi-shagun-scheme-registration/
7. https://pib.gov.in/PressReleasePage.aspx?PRID=1812756
8. https://economictimes.indiatimes.com/news/politics-and-nation/bjp-promises-to-senior-citizens-a-trip-to-jerusalem-in-nagaland-poll-manifesto/articleshow/62962346.cms?from=mdr

9. https://legislative.gov.in/constitution-forty-second-amendment-act-1976
10. https://epaper.thehindu.com/ccidist-ws/th/th_delhi/issues/20322/OPS/GB5AN3NB4.1+G4HAN45EM.1.html
11. https://www.indiacode.nic.in/bitstream/123456789/13275/1/TNHR%26CE%20ACT%2C%201959%20-%20revised%20and%20updated.pdf; https://swarajyamag.com/magazine/this-model-legislation-will-take-the-government-out-of-our-temples
12. https://www.newindianexpress.com/states/tamil-nadu/2020/sep/10/madras-hc-refuses-to-entertain-plea-challenging-tamil-nadus-law-on-hindu-temples-2195108.html
13. https://www.thehindu.com/todays-paper/tp-national/sc-notice-to-ap-on-petition-challenging-hr-and-ce-act/article4211676.ece
14. https://www.indiccollective.org/wp-content/uploads/2020/01/Writ-Petition-for-Tiruchendur.pdf
15. https://theprint.in/opinion/indian-govt-wont-be-any-different-from-british-if-hindus-cant-manage-their-own-temples/218210/
16. http://cms.tn.gov.in/sites/default/files/documents/HR_and%20_CE.pdf
17. https://itms.kar.nic.in/hrcehome/index.php
18. https://indianexpress.com/article/explained/indu-malhotra-padmanabhaswamy-temple-case-kerala-temple-affairs-explained-8121405/
19. https://www.livelaw.in/pdf_upload/2157002967020224230221105848-1-460077.pdf

20. https://www.indiccollective.org/wp-content/uploads/2021/04/W.P.-No.-14256-of-2020.pdf
21. https://indictales.com/2019/08/07/how-do-we-administer-our-temples-a-talk-by-tr-ramesh/
22. https://theprint.in/opinion/indian-govt-wont-be-any-different-from-british-if-hindus-cant-manage-their-own-temples/218210/
23. https://inmathi.com/2021/09/20/kapaleeswarar-temple-land-471-defaulters-40-per-cent-annual-revenue-loss/25079/
24. https://www.news18.com/news/politics/bjp-slams-mamatas-decision-to-appoint-muslim-leader-as-head-of-tarakeshwar-development-board-1438087.html
25. https://www.deccanherald.com/national/christian-mla-on-ttd-trust-board-spurs-row-665948.html
26. http://www.bareactslive.com/MP/MP728.HTM
27. https://www.deccanchronicle.com/nation/current-affairs/101022/tirumala-temple-gets-hundi-collection-of-rs-78269-crore-in-six-months.html
28. https://www.timesnownews.com/india/tirumala-venkateswaras-properties-are-worth-rs-85705-crore-tdd-reveals-wealth-details-article-94447297
29. https://www.thehindu.com/news/national/andhra-pradesh/high-court-reprieve-to-temples-having-annual-income-of-up-to-5-lakh/article65411049.ece
30. https://www.newindianexpress.com/states/andhra-pradesh/2022/aug/17/government-forms-21-member-andhra-pradesh-dharmika-parishad-2488378.html

31. https://www.thehindu.com/news/national/tamil-nadu/11999-temples-have-no-revenue-to-perform-puja-hrce-tells-madras-high-court/article32127028.ece
32. https://www.reuters.com/world/india/indias-jammu-kashmir-receives-most-tourists-75-years-2022-10-07/
33. https://indianexpress.com/article/india/about-5700-rohingya-muslims-residing-in-jammu-and-kashmir-mehbooba-mufti-4483711/
34. https://theprint.in/features/locked-up-like-animals-pandits-want-to-flee-kashmir-hope-its-their-last-exodus/988337/
35. https://www.thehindu.com/news/national/only-17-of-proposed-accommodation-for-kashmiri-migrants-built-so-far-show-home-ministry-data/article65241269.ece
36. https://indianexpress.com/article/political-pulse/kashmiri-pandits-pm-modi-job-package-secure-areas-7920765/
37. https://www.mha.gov.in/sites/default/files/2022-08/StatusVariousSchemes_06062017%5B1%5D.pdf
38. https://www.business-standard.com/article/news-ians/12-years-on-nadimarg-massacre-still-rankles-ians-feature-115032300908_1.html
39. https://english.jagran.com/entertainment/the-kashmir-files-who-was-girija-tickoo-the-kashmiri-pandit-woman-who-was-raped-and-killed-with-carpenter-saw-10040986
40. https://newsable.asianetnews.com/india/the-kashmir-files-eyewitness-accoubt-kashmiri-pandit-exodus-r935ob

41. http://www.indiandefencereview.com/news/kashmiri-pandits-offered-three-choices-by-radical-islamists/
42. https://www.tribuneindia.com/news/j-k/yasin-malik-should-not-have-roamed-freely-for-32-years-wife-of-slain-iaf-officer-398069
43. https://www.news18.com/news/india/bitta-karate-butcher-of-kashmiri-pandits-admitted-to-killings-on-video-31-yrs-on-he-faces-a-murder-trial-4922849.html
44. https://indianexpress.com/article/india/kashmiri-pandits-killings-supreme-court-refuses-to-reopen-215-cases/
45. https://www.deccanherald.com/national/north-and-central/supreme-court-dismisses-curative-petition-for-probe-into-genocide-of-kashmiri-pandits-1169824.html
46. https://www.jstor.org/stable/25742155
47. https://www.independent.co.uk/news/world/asia/china-re-education-muslims-ramadan-xinjiang-eat-pork-alcohol-communist-xi-jinping-a8357966.html
48. https://www.outlookindia.com/national/j-k-police-says-88-percent-drop-in-law-and-order-incidents-in-kashmir-since-article-370-abrogation-news-214371
49. https://www.pib.gov.in/PressReleasePage.aspx?PRID=1776816
50. https://twitter.com/AdityaRajKaul/status/689317273337610241?ref_src=twsrc%5Etfw%7Ctwcamp%5Etweetembed%7Ctwterm%5E689317273337610241%7Ctwgr%5Eea4e3869452b057d035b9e5ba770a896b65762b6%7Ctwcon%5Es1_&ref_url=https%3A%2F%2Fwww.indiatoday.in%2Ffyi%2Fstory%2Fexodus-of-kashmiri-pandits-january-19-jammu-and-kashmir-304487-2016-01-19

51. https://theprint.in/opinion/waqf-boards-are-indias-big-urban-landlords-but-whose-interest-are-they-serving/1430928/
52. https://lawbeat.in/columns/waqf-land-legal-interpretations-political-strategy
53. https://www.milligazette.com/news/2-focus/10114-return-of-123-waqf-properties-no-reason-to-rejoice/
54. https://www.deccanherald.com/content/31093/in-name-allah-waqf-corruption.html
55. https://www.timesnownews.com/videos/times-now/india-upfront/why-did-congress-gift-prestigious-properties-to-waqf-board-india-upfront-english-news-video-94253621
56. https://www.milligazette.com/news/2-focus/10114-return-of-123-waqf-properties-no-reason-to-rejoice/
57. https://www.milligazette.com/news/2-focus/10114-return-of-123-waqf-properties-no-reason-to-rejoice/
58. http://archive.indianexpress.com/news/wakf-chief-who-stood-in-way-of-ambani-s-dream-home-shunted-out/305947/
59. https://www.wamsi.nic.in/wamsi/dashBoardAction.do;jsessionid=5A04636BD1E2F73B244D-62CF45E9DC4F?method=totalRegisteredProp
60. https://www.wamsi.nic.in/wamsi/legis/SCJudgement_OnceWaqfAlwaysWaqf.pdf
61. http://www.mpwaqfboard.org/Public%20Page/WhatisWaqf.aspx
62. https://indianexpress.com/article/explained/explained-how-a-waqf-is-created-and-the-laws-that-govern-such-properties-6072476/

63. https://legislative.gov.in/sites/default/files/A1995-43.pdf
64. https://legislative.gov.in/sites/default/files/A1995-43.pdf
65. https://www.indiacode.nic.in/show-data?actid=AC_CEN_44_74_00001_199543_1517807323904&sectionId=10398&sectionno=54&orderno=56
66. https://legislative.gov.in/sites/default/files/A1995-43.pdf
67. https://www.livelaw.in/top-stories/wakf-tribunal-to-try-suit-when-dispute-is-whether-property-is-wakf-or-not-142722
68. https://legal.economictimes.indiatimes.com/news/industry/law-cannot-be-challenged-in-abstract-says-sc-refuses-to-entertain-plea-against-waqf-act/90838569
69. https://www.livelaw.in/top-stories/supreme-court-refuses-to-entertain-plea-challenging-wakf-act-196545
70. https://legislative.gov.in/sites/default/files/A1995-43.pdf
71. https://legislative.gov.in/sites/default/files/A1995-43.pdf
72. https://www.thehindu.com/news/national/other-states/gyanvapi-is-waqf-property-mosque-committee-tells-court/article65803233.ece#:~:text=The%20committee%20informed%20the%20court,any%20matter%20pertaining%20to%20it
73. https://ianslive.in/news/tn_waqf_board_claims_ownership_of_1500_year_old_temple_land-906080/NATION/1
74. https://www.wamsi.nic.in/wamsi/legis/PM_Letter_26March1976.pdf

NOTES AND REFERENCES

75. https://www.wamsi.nic.in/wamsi/legis/Waqf_EvictionBill2014_RS_Eng.pdf
76. http://www.columbia.edu/itc/mealac/pritchett/00ambedkar/ambedkar_partition/412b.html
77. https://timesofindia.indiatimes.com/blogs/myview/waqf-act1995-a-tool-given-to-waqf-boards-to-snatch-the-property-of-hindus/
78. https://www.indiatoday.in/law/story/idgah-maidan-ganesh-chaturthi-bengaluru-karnataka-waqf-board-supreme-court-1993814-2022-08-29
79. https://legislative.gov.in/sites/default/files/The%20Right%20of%20Children%20to%20Free%20and%20Compulsory%20Education%20Act,%202009.pdf
80. https://tfipost.com/2017/01/rte-act-assault-hindu-run-institutions/
81. https://tfipost.com/2017/01/rte-act-assault-hindu-run-institutions/
82. https://swarajyamag.com/ideas/how-hindu-rights-have-been-seriously-damaged-by-article-30-and-rte-act
83. https://www.sadhana108.com/2017/07/11/hindu-schools-closing-right-education-law-rte/
84. https://swarajyamag.com/ideas/how-hindu-rights-have-been-seriously-damaged-by-article-30-and-rte-act
85. https://intellectualkshatriya.com/indias-veda-phobic-educational-system-constitutionalhinduphobia/
86. https://swarajyamag.com/politics/the-right-to-education-act-in-two-cheat-sheets-problems-and-possible-solutions

87. https://www.youtube.com/watch?v=ZUcDp3wsd4E
88. https://www.thenewsminute.com/article/nps-controversy-rte-sectarian-legislation-which-needs-be-repealed-49712
89. https://nisaindia.org/data-on-school-closures
90. https://sundayguardianlive.com/news/11613-rte-leading-closure-low-budget-private-schools
91. https://www.educationworld.in/why-the-rte-act-should-be-scrapped/
92. https://www.dnaindia.com/education/report-7000-maharashtra-schools-served-closure-notice-due-to-non-compliance-of-rte-norms-2293511
93. https://cof.org/sites/default/files/documents/files/India/The%20Constitution%20of%20India%20Article%2030.pdf
94. https://www.constitutionofindia.net/constitution_of_india/fundamental_rights/articles/Article%2028
95. https://indiankanoon.org/doc/1858991/
96. https://www.constitutionofindia.net/constitution_of_india/fundamental_rights/articles/Article%2015
97. https://www.india.gov.in/sites/upload_files/npi/files/amend93.pdf?fbclid%E2%80%89=%E2%80%89IwAR33t3LPSmFiiOrPTReOneb3PHKjjx2aDmuny7DuBcptSGA7U3i-asQKAV0
98. https://timesofindia.indiatimes.com/city/mumbai/rte-row-4000-schools-to-stay-shut-on-monday/articleshow/68121019.cms
99. https://timesofindia.indiatimes.com/business/india-business/cag-finds-deficiencies-in-rte-act-implementation-in-haryana/articleshow/57397146.cms

100. https://ccs.in/reimbursements-under-rte-section-122-too-little-too-late
101. https://www.livemint.com/Sundayapp/qHoFCwxUpOdaEesYFA2h2K/Its-time-to-reform-the-RTE-Act.html
102. https://www.hindustantimes.com/india-news/supreme-court-seeks-govt-report-on-minority-status-for-hindus-by-august-30-101652208629150.html
103. https://www.indialegallive.com/magazine/hindus-minority-tag-ministry-of-minority-affairs-ashwini-kumar-upadhyay/
104. https://www.indiatoday.in/news-analysis/story/minority-status-hindus-centre-approach-1947725-2022-05-10
105. https://indiankanoon.org/doc/508426/
106. https://indiankanoon.org/doc/1188494/
107. https://prsindia.org/files/bills_acts/bills_parliament/2005/NAC_Draft_Communal_Violence_Bill_2011.pdf
108. https://www.business-standard.com/article/economy-policy/nac-s-communal-violence-prevention-bill-the-fine-print-111091800053_1.html
109. https://quran.com/en/an-nisa/11
110. https://www.indiatoday.in/india/story/muslim-girl-marriageable-age-15-years-or-puberty-gujarat-high-court-230038-2014-12-06
111. https://www.sociolegalreview.com/post/criminalisation-of-triple-talaq-dissecting-the-constitutional-and-socio-legal-aspects
112. https://www.youtube.com/watch?v=_NAp2kHIzc4&t=2s

113. https://www.timesnownews.com/india/article/lok-sabha-passes-bill-to-remove-leprosy-as-ground-for-divorce/343169
114. https://www.tribuneindia.com/news/archive/j-k/news-detail-773637
115. https://www.business-standard.com/about/what-is-uniform-civil-code
116. https://mea.gov.in/Images/attach/amb/Volume_14_01.pdf
117. http://www.columbia.edu/itc/mealac/pritchett/00ambedkar/ambedkar_partition/410.html
118. https://indiankanoon.org/doc/823221/
119. http://www.anandranganathan.com/2013/09/05/inconvenient-judgments/
120. https://legislative.gov.in/sites/default/files/A1986-25_1.pdf
121. https://sunnah.com/bukhari:5134
122. https://sunnah.com/nasai:3378
123. https://www.hindustantimes.com/india-news/arrogance-clout-sc-slams-nupur-sharma-over-prophet-remarks-what-court-said-101656655590409.html
124. https://indianexpress.com/article/india/sabarimala-verdict-justice-indu-malhotra-dissents-cant-invoke-rationality-in-religion-5378873/
125. https://timesofindia.indiatimes.com/travel/destinations/5-temples-in-india-where-men-are-not-allowed/photostory/83956698.cms
126. https://swarajyamag.com/culture/the-sabarimala-review-and-articles-of-faith-and-rationality
127. https://www.youtube.com/watch?v=_5gw03e85Ik

128. https://www.livelaw.in/top-stories/tripura-hc-bans-animal-bird-sacrifice-in-temples-148529#:~:text=Constitution%20of%20India.-,No%20person%20including%20the%20State%20shall%20be%20allowed%20to%20sacrifice,Karol%20and%20Justice%20Arindam%20Lodh
129. https://www.hindustantimes.com/punjab/no-animal-sacrifice-during-kullu-dussehra-rakesh-kanwar/story-1mX8xo9atOfggxbcDEXFTM.html
130. https://indianexpress.com/article/india/ngt-bans-chanting-of-mantras-ringing-of-bells-in-amarnath-temple-4980926/
131. https://swarajyamag.com/commentary/supreme-court-wont-ban-halal-slaughter-but-the-govt-must-many-european-countries-have-already-done-so
132. https://timesofindia.indiatimes.com/city/delhi/krishna-stole-butter-but-he-never-did-any-acrobatics-sc/articleshow/53749819.cms
133. https://aaqr.org/articles/aaqr-13-01-oa-0031.pdf
134. https://www.downtoearth.org.in/blog/agriculture/stubble-burning-a-problem-for-the-environment-agriculture-and-humans-64912
135. https://theicct.org/wp-content/uploads/2022/05/Meta-study-India-transport_final.pdf
136. https://www.ncbi.nlm.nih.gov/pmc/articles/PMC6693810/pdf/dyz022.pdf
137. https://www.thehindu.com/news/cities/Tiruchirapalli/ban-order-issued-for-dharmapuram-adheenams-pattina-pravesam/article65378679.ece

138. https://www.thelancet.com/journals/lancet/article/PIIS0140-6736(02)07737-1/fulltext
139. https://www.hindustantimes.com/india-news/cant-deny-non-hindus-right-to-do-business-near-temples-top-court-101639766460154.html
140. https://www.census2011.co.in/data/town/801381-bakhtiarpur-bihar.html
141. https://bharatabharati.in/2014/08/26/
142. https://indianexpress.com/article/opinion/columns/how-history-was-made-up-at-nalanda/
143. https://www.google.co.in/books/edition/Babur_Nama/VW2HJL689wgC?hl=en&gbpv=1&dq=baburnama&printsec=frontcover
144. https://swarajyamag.com/ideas/as-icons-of-colonialism-fall-across-the-globe-india-must-also-reassess-its-cultural-heroes-uncover-their-misdeeds-and-retell-history
145. https://www.google.co.in/books/edition/Kashmir_and_It_s_People/QpjKpK7ywPIC?hl=en&gbpv=1&dq=inauthor:%22M.+K.+Kaw%22&printsec=frontcover
146. https://swarajyamag.com/politics/chadar-at-ajmer-sharif-and-praises-on-prithviraj-chauhan-cannot-go-hand-in-hand-chishti-blessed-ghori-to-defeat-prithviraj-as-per-his-biography
147. https://www.firstpost.com/living/aurangzebs-tyranny-and-bigotry-cannot-be-whitewashed-a-counter-view-3426630.html
148. https://www.hindustantimes.com/columns/the-way-backward-and-a-way-forward/story-aKEpOpWAngQybRTpFqL6EP.html

149. https://www.firstpost.com/opinion-news-expert-views-news-analysis-firstpost-viewpoint/whitewashing-genocides-and-history-phobia-why-ks-lals-claims-of-80-mn-hindus-killed-by-islamic-barbarism-hold-water-11618501.html
150. https://ia802706.us.archive.org/4/items/selectlettersoft00tipu/selectlettersoft00tipu.pdf
151. https://www.amazon.in/Major-General-Thomas-Munro-Governor-Madras/dp/1295525550
152. https://www.google.co.in/books/edition/Mysore_a_Gazetteer_Compiled_for_Governme/EO6FzQEACAAJ?hl=en
153. https://www.google.co.in/books/edition/Tipu_Sultan/Ma05AQAAIAAJ?hl=en&gbpv=1&bsq=-Colonel+R.D.+Palsokar&dq=Colonel+R.D.+Palsokar&printsec=frontcover
154. https://timesofindia.indiatimes.com/city/bengaluru/mandyam-community-still-feels-tipus-sword/articleshow/71861480.cms
155. https://legislative.gov.in/sites/default/files/A1991-42.pdf
156. https://www.sci.gov.in/pdf/JUD_2.pdf
157. https://www.nytimes.com/2020/06/09/world/europe/king-leopold-statue-antwerp.html
158. https://openthemagazine.com/cover-stories/where-did-the-temples-go/
159. https://openthemagazine.com/cover-stories/where-did-the-temples-go/
160. https://www.indiafacts.org.in/ayodhya-dispute-fighting-eminent-historians/

161. https://www.nature.com/articles/337611a0
162. https://openthemagazine.com/cover-stories/aurangzebs-reign-in-the-light-of-his-own-orders/
163. https://archive.org/details/in.ernet.dli.2015.62691
164. https://timesofindia.indiatimes.com/india/rss-chief-why-look-for-shivling-in-every-mosque/articleshow/91971714.cms
165. https://www.hindustanbooks.com/pdfs/10120488-Hindu-TemplesWhat-Happend-to-Them-by-Sita-Ram-Goel.pdf
166. https://www.opindia.com/2022/02/hindus-will-lose-out-if-ucc-brought-without-preparations-adv-j-sai-deepak/
167. https://www.youtube.com/watch?v=lYXX6vj0fmQ

Acknowledgements

I would like to thank Mr Mrugank Paranjape and the Probodhan Manch, Vile Parle, from whose stage my lecture, 'Hindus in Hindu Rashtra', was delivered. I thank my publisher Praveen Tewari and editor Arnab Karmakar. Without their expert guidance, this work would not have seen the light of day. I thank Alo Pal for critical reading of the manuscript. Some passages, for example the ones that elaborate on the Shah Bano and the Sabarimala cases, have been taken from articles published previously by me and they can be found on *www.anandranganathan.com*. This work has been passed through the Turnitin software.

Above all, I would like to thank the Hindus of this great country who continue to suffer so much discrimination and still manage to keep up appearances with a sprightly smile on their face and a bounce in their step. And so just this once, I am willing to let go of my Darwinian beliefs and hope that this thing called Karma exists and it brings to them what is long overdue—justice, equality, parity. As a small gesture of my appreciation and gratitude towards this all-accepting, long-suffering, uncomplaining, perhaps to the point of meekness, community, all royalties due to me from this work will go to the Hindu refugee cause.

Index

A
Abdullah, Farook, 21
Agnihotri, Vivek, 13
AIMPLB, 59
Allahabad High Court, 100
Andhra Pradesh Hindu Religious Institutions Act, 8
Anita, Vangalapudi, 6
Ardhanareswara Temple, 4
Armed Forces, 108
Attukal Bhagavathy Temple, 71
Ayodhya Judgment, 93, 95, 100
Ayyappa Temples, 71

B
Babri Masjid–Ram Janambhoomi
case, 94
issue, 98
Babri mosque, 99
Bano, Shah, 61-62, 66
Bhagwat, Mohan, 102
BJP, 19
B.N. Rau Committee, 59
Bose, Subhas Chandra, 106
Brahmaji Temple, 71
Buddhist shrine, 99

C
Central Vista, 27
CGO Complex, 27
Charitable Endowments Act, 2
Chief Executive Officer, 32, 36
Chief Justice of India, 36
Civil Code, 63
Code of Criminal Procedure, 62
Communal Violence Bill, 56
Cultural and Educational Rights, 48
Cultural heritage, 81

D
Delhi High Court, 27, 28
District Magistrate, 36
Durant, Will, 84

E
Election Commission, 106
EWS quota, 50

G
Gandhi, Sonia, 56
Gangasagar, 108
Goa inquisition, 82
Goel, Sitaram, 102
Guha, Ramchandra, 84
Guru Tegh Bahadur, 84, 86
Gyanwapi Mosque, 38, 92, 101

H
Hakim, Firhad, 6
High court, 8
Hindu
 community, 56
 educational institutions, 45
 laws, 59
 Muslim unity, 94
 Rashtra, 7, 22, 30, 44, 45, 46, 54, 91, 100, 107
 refugees, 41
 temples, 84, 101
Hindu Religious Institutions Act, 8
Hindu Society, 60
Hindu Code Bills, 59
Hindu festivals
 diwali, 76
 jallikattu, 75
 kambala, 75
 makar sankranti, 75
 nagapanchami, 75
Hinduism, 55, 60, 67

I
Indian law, 56
Indian Trusts Act, 31
Indo-US nuclear deal, 88
IPC sections, 55
Islamic
 scriptures, 67
 state, 18
 system, 18

J
Jaiswal, Suvira, 99
Janata Dal, 19
Jawaharlal Nehru Stadium, 27

K
Kamakhya Temple, 71
Kapaleeswarar Temple, 5
Kapoor, Kareena, 84
Kashi Vishwanath Temple, 38, 85, 103

Kashmiri Hindus, 12, 15, 16, 22, 23, 25, 26
  activist, 23
  refugees, 13
Kaul, Aditya Raj, 23
Khan, Saif Ali, 85
Khwaja Moinuddin Chishti, 83
Kumari Amman Temple, 71

L
Lal, K.S., 84
Limitation Act, 37
Lord Shiva, 70
Lucknow Museum, 99

M
Madras High Court, 8
Madras Regulation, 2
Mahakaleshwar Mandir Act, 7
Mahakaleshwar Temple, 7
Mander, Harsh, 57
Manendiyavalli Chandrashekhara Swami Temple, 38
Masir-e-Alamgiri, 38, 101
Mata Temple, 71
Miri, Sikandar Shah, 83
Modi, Narendra, 83
Moharram, 75, 76, 78
Moinuddin Chishti, 83
Mughal Emperor, 84
Muslim
  community, 63
  personal law, 56, 62
  society, 61
Muslim Women Protection of Rights on Divorce Act 1986, 65

N
Nalanda, 80, 81
National Commission for Minorities Educational Institutions (NCMEI), 52
National Commission for Minority Education Institutions, 52
Nava-e-Hurriyat, 17
NCMEI Act, 52

P
Patel, Sardar, 20
Places of Worship Act, 91, 92, 94, 100, 102
Prevention of Communal and Targeted Violence, 56
Prohibition of Child Marriage Act, 58

Q
Quran, 70, 71, 79

R
Raman, C.V., 106
Ramesh, T.R., 5
Ram Janambhoomi, 91, 97
Religious Endowments Act, 2
Religious Institutions and Charitable Endowments Act, 8
Rent Control Acts, 39
Right to Education Act, 43
Rohingya Muslims, 11
Roy, Arundhati, 25
RTE Act, 43
RTE rules, 53
Rushdie, Salman, 22

S
Sabarimala verdict, 69, 70
Sahih al-Bukhari, 67
Sampath, Vikram, 103
Saraswati, Swami Dayananda, 3, 4
Scheduled Castes, 49, 50, 57
Scheduled Tribes, 49, 50, 57
Sharma, Nupur, 59, 67, 68
Shia Waqf, 29, 31
Shirur Mutt Judgment, 73
Societies Registration Act, 31
Srivastava, Sushil, 100
State-sanctioned hypocrisy, 59
Sunni Waqf, 31
Supreme Court, 3, 7, 16, 29, 35, 36, 58, 62, 65, 66, 69, 70, 93, 100

T
The Kashmir Files, 13, 15, 23
Triple Talaq, 59
Tripura High Court, 73

U
Union Minister of Home Affairs, 97
Upadhyay, Ashwini Kumar, 35, 52

V
Vishnu Hari inscription, 99

W
Wakf Board, 39
Waqf Act, 27, 30, 35, 36, 40
Waqf Boards, 28, 29, 30, 36, 39, 66
Waqf Estate Officer, 40

Waqf Eviction Officer, 40
Waqf land, 27, 28, 38
Waqf Management
    System of India, 29

Waqf property, 32, 34, 39

Y
Yadav, Akhilesh, 85